Jews in Early Mississippi

Publication of this book was made possible in part
with the generous assistance of the American Jewish
Archives and the Phil Hardin Foundation.

Jews in Early Mississippi

by
Rabbi Leo E. Turitz
and
Evelyn Turitz

UNIVERSITY PRESS OF MISSISSIPPI
Jackson

ACKNOWLEDGMENTS

This venture in history in photographic form calling for many sources would have been totally impossible without the cooperation of many people and we are deeply indebted to each one for his or her part in helping it come to fruition.

We single out here at the very beginning Albert W. Herzog who, from the very inception of this study, provided encouragement in one form or another.

Since neither one of the authors had any experience in photography, it was necessary to turn to experts in order to acquire the needed skills. Cecil Adkins of Meridian, an excellent teacher of photography, was most helpful with special problems. Jerry Stokes, teacher and professional Meridian photographer, was cooperative beyond the usual call of business.

Librarians, archivists, and researchers whom we approached for assistance understood the merit of the research and graciously made materials and information accessible. We thank each one of them.

Of the American Jewish Archives in Cincinnati there were Dr. Jacob R. Marcus, director, and dean of American Jewish historians who has "raised up many disciples"; Dr. Abraham J. Peck, associate director; and Fanny Zelcer, archivist.

Of the Mississippi Department of Archives and History there were Elbert Hilliard, director; Patti Carr Black, museum director; Madel Morgan, archives director; Jody Cook, research specialist; and Stephen F. Young, museum curator.

Of the Meridian Public Library there were Mary Earle Smith, James S. Progar, and Kay Thompson who made "The Mississippi Room" and other facilities of the library available to us.

Other Mississippi librarians who aided our research were: *McComb*, Frances G. Wilber and Anne Hoff; *Natchez*; Elenora Gralow; *Pontotoc*, Elliott Thompson; and *Brookhaven*, Rebecca Nations.

In other parts of the country there were: Dr. Malcolm H. Stern, past president of the American Society of Genealogists, New York; Dr. Louis Schmier, Southern Historical Society, Valdosta, Georgia; Lori Feldman, librarian, Hebrew Union College library, Cincinnati; and Rabbi Martin M. Weitz, Laguna Hills, California, veteran journal editor, who made helpful suggestions.

Two newspaper editors were most cooperative. They are Edgar T. Crisler, Jr., of the *Post Gibson Reveille*, and John S. Lewis, of the *Woodville Republican*. Angela Haymes Rutherford of the Columbus newspaper was most helpful.

Rabbi Sidney Strome, Greenville; Rabbi Richard J. Birnholz, Jackson; Rabbi Allan H. Schwartzman, Vicksburg; Mr. Morris Rozolsky, president of the Natchez temple; and Mayor Harold Samuels, Brookhaven, facilitated our visits to their respective communities.

Those who contributed photographs and provided accompanying information are acknowledged in conjunction with items shown in the course of the book.

In addition, we wish to thank the following people for assisting in a variety of ways: *Brookhaven*, Clifford Abrams; *Canton*, Alice Stein; *Greenville*, David Davidow, Rachel Baskind, Max Weinstein, Rosalie Rafael; *Indianola*, Morris Lewis, Jr., Celian Lewis; *Jackson*, Lolita Cohen, Dr. Julian Wiener, Dr. Eugene Hesdorffer, Celeste Orkin, Phyllis Herman, Harold G. Gotthelf, Jr., Fred Marks; *Lexington*, Fay Berman, Irma Paris, Eugene Herman, Herbert Hyman; *Meridian*, A. L. and Joan Cahn, Mayor Alfred and Lucile Rosenbaum, Lewis Rosenbaum, Clarice Ullman, William and Dorothy Lerner, William and Diane Lerner, Sam and Doris Feltenstein, Libby Dumont, Sara Niemetz, Frances Davidson, Harold and Ruth Meyer, Harold and Helen Meyer, Sam and Ruth Davidson, Marty and Linda Davidson, William and Sarah Goldberger, Morris and Eve Kogon, Max and Ida Mushlin, Robert and Arlene Merson, Rhoda Herzog; *Natchez*, Elaine Lehmann, Abe Geisenberger, Delphine Tillman, Naomi Lehman, George and Bernice Abrams, Zelda Millstein; *Port Gibson*, Bertha Anderson; *Summit*, David and Dolores Feldman; *Vicksburg*, Frieda Fischel, Carolyn Leyens Meyer, Richard P. Marcus, Isadore Marcus, Mr. and Mrs. Sam Kleisdorf, Ann Emmich, Jack S. Rice; *Woodville*, Mary B. Scott.

Out of state: Barbara Levy, West Newton, Mass.; Rabbi Fred V. Davidow, Atlanta, Ga.; Mildred Kern, Baltimore, Md.; Margaret Pearlstein, Newport Beach, Ca.; Madeline Gottlieb, Davenport, Ia.; Jane Mason, Bethesda, Md.; Edwin J. Feiler, Savannah, Ga.; Isabel Goldman, Shreveport, La.; Samuel Willner, Baltimore, Md.; Herbert M. Meyer, Detroit, Mich.; Ninna Harris Smith, Monroe, La.; Ellis Titche, Dallas, Texas; Henry B. Philippsborn, Dallas; Evelyn R. Rosenblum, Steubenville, Ohio; Barbaree Heaster, Bridgeport, W. Va.

New Orleans, Louisiana: Mrs. Harry Greenberg, Daniel L. Scharff, Dan S. Scharff, Jr., Frank Friedler, Emily Benjamin, Richard Lowenberg, Lynette Fried, and Rose Rich.

Second edition copyright © 1995 by the University Press of Mississippi
All rights reserved
First published 1983 by the University Press of Mississippi
Manufactured in the United States of America
98 97 96 95   4 3 2 1
The paper in this book meets the guidelines for permanence and durability of the Committee on Production Guidelines for Book Longevity of the Council on Library Resources.

British Library Cataloging-in-Publication data available
The Cataloging-in-Publication information is for the first edition also.
Library of Congress Cataloging in Publication Data

Turitz, Leo.
    Jews in early Mississippi.

    Bibliography: p.
    Includes index.
    1. Jews—Mississippi—History—19th century.
2. Mississippi—Ethnic relations—History—19th century.   I. Turitz, Evelyn.   II. Title.
F350.J5T87   1983   976.2'004924   82-25093
ISBN 0-87805-178-3

Contents

Foreword

It is a most pleasant task and a cherished privilege to be asked by Rabbi Leo E. Turitz and his dear wife Evelyn to write a foreword to their new edition of *Jews in Early Mississippi*. There was a time when Southern Jewry was more important culturally and religiously than the New York Jewish community. This was in the brief generation of the 1790s to the early 1820s, a generation inspired by young intellectuals who gave birth to the Reformed Society of Israelites. Decades later the Civil War destroyed the spiritual and intellectual life of Southern Jewry even as it exacted its toll of the larger general community. The Jews of the South—many of them notables—fled to New Orleans, Washington, New York, and even to distant California.

In her highly impressionistic but very readable account of the "Mind of Mississippi," native daughter Gayle Graham Yates does not hesitate, despite her obvious love of the state, to tell her reader that "in the world's opinion, Mississippi is probably one of the most despised of all places in the United States."[1] Mississippi is, according to the author, "an easy scapegoat in American society, for it readily exhibits the sins of the nation—poverty, prejudice, racism, sexism, war, arrogance, narrow-mindedness, both religious and political fanaticism. . . ."[2]

It is not an easy image to live with, this picture of a place that is often depicted as more backward than any other in its region of the southern United States. Yet even those Mississippians who have benefitted least from establishing historical roots in its soil display an uncommon love for certain parts of it. Among them is James Meredith, the African-American political activist who in his student days at the University of Mississippi single-handedly destroyed the system of segregation at "Ole Miss":[3]

> I can love Mississippi because of the beauty of the countryside and the old traditions of family affection, and for such small things as flowers bursting in spring and the way you can see for miles from a ridge in winter.
>
> Why should a Negro be forced to leave such things? Because of fear? No. Not anymore.

The faces in Leo E. and Evelyn Turitz's *Jews in Early Mississippi* also do not reflect fear and why should they? The European Jews who came to America in the first part of the nineteenth century found a land of expansive capitalism, dynamic and largely successful. They found a nation whose golden age lay not in a medievalized past of corporate political structures, but in a political tradition reflective basically of an optimistic, idealistic view of people and government. To a people who historically had been denied the fruits of full equality in the lands of their birth, who had suffered economic and professional as well as geographic restrictions and had always been on the margin of national activity, it was like entering heaven.

Entering Mississippi in the 1840s may have been a little less heavenly. Like much of the South, it was an "armed camp," as the South Carolina Jewish writer Ludwig Lewisohn once described it. These early Jews would find a newly established planter class, a group of plantation owners and slavekeepers who "still ate dinner in shirt sleeves and washed on the back porch and let the chickens roost in the top of the trees in the yard."[4]

It may be that the plantation owner saw in the Jewish peddlers who came to the South a mirror image of himself, of the Southern man on the make, overcoming hurdle after hurdle, in order to succeed at business.

Plantation owners were ensconced in an agrarian tradition wedded to the cultivation of staple crops—tobacco, sugar cane, rice, and cotton. The welcome given to the immigrant Jew from Germany was enthusiastic for a very clear reason: Jews represented a numerically and politically powerless substitute for the independent middle-class feared by the plantation owners as a potential rival for economic and political power.

These newly arrived Jews were basically unobtrusive and interested in making a living. They fit very well into the political and social pattern established by the Southern planter elite. Their sense of civic responsibility and social consciousness paralleled that of the southern elite. And the Jews were grateful for the religious and economic benefits they derived from the system in which they lived.

Did it matter so much why they were welcome in Mississippi? Where else would members of the Christian community donate monies to help build the local synagogue? Where else could Jews be members of the city council or even become mayor? Where else, as in the case of Leopold Marks, could a town be named after a Jew?

And when it came time to answer the call to arms, the Jews of Mississippi went with enthusiasm. And when it came time to mourn for the Lost Cause, that, too, became part of their civic duty.

It did not matter if after the end of the Civil War the ease and informality which had marked the antebellum relationship between Jews and Christians was more difficult to maintain. One reason for the changed atmosphere after 1865 was the growing anti-modernist impulse in Southern Protestant evangelical circles. Theological conservatism and the revivalist evangelicalism of the early nineteenth century South enjoyed a renascence at the end of the 1870s and into the next decade. Conservative Protestant ministers attacked Judaism as a "relic of the dark ages," paralleling the outbreaks of anti-Semitic "whitecapping" in Mississippi at about the same time.[5]

But for most of the Jews in this volume, these would be events that would not shake their love of and devotion to the state of Mississippi. Yet one must ask: what did they think as they listened to a Friday night or Saturday morning sermon in their local temple as the rabbi interpreted the Reform Jewish concern with prophetic justice? What did they think as they left the service with the rabbi's call for social justice still ringing in their ears and entered the "real world" of social separation and disenfranchisement of African Americans? Did they think of themselves as a part of that world?

These are only some of the questions that need to be explored. The South today includes about twenty percent of the country's Jews, and the study of the Southern Jewish experience is rapidly emerging as a legitimate and exciting part of Southern history. Years ago Bertram Wallace Korn set out to chronicle, in part, the Jews of the South. His history of early New Orleans is a beautiful piece of scholarship, meticulous, informative, readable. The South, imposing in its numbers, is now beginning to catch up scholastically. There are all-day schools where Hebrew is taught; regional universities have established Jewish studies departments. Scholars are addressing themselves to the adventures of the Jews in the States below the Mason-Dixon Line. Doctoral candidates are working on important dissertations, and first-rate articles and monographs are beginning to appear.

If there is to be an authentic history of American Jewry it must do more than acknowl-

edge the importance of the national Jewish organizations centered in New York City; it must
build from the ground up, state by state. We are
grateful to Leo E. and Evelyn Turitz, for this is
what they are doing. They are pioneers resurrect-
ing the past in an act of "loving kindness," a bow
to their forefathers. Once Mississippi sheltered
6400 Jews; today they number but 1400 souls.
Jews in Early Mississippi is a brave, bold, and
successful attempt to breathe new life into a
world that has vanished. We as historians are
deeply grateful for this essential research tool for
scholars of Southern and Mississippi Jewish history. Future generations, too, will rise up and call
them blessed.

Jacob R. Marcus and Abraham J. Peck
American Jewish Archives
Hebrew Union College—Jewish Institute of
Religion

[1] Gayle Graham Yates, *Mississippi Mind: A Personal Cultural History of an American State* (Knoxville: University of Tennessee Press, 1990), p. 11.

[2] Ibid.

[3] Ibid., p. 13.

[4] Bertram Wyatt-Brown, "W.J. Cash and Southern Culture," in *From the Old South to the New: Essays on the Transitional South*, ed. Walter J. Fraser, Jr. and Winfred B. Moore, Jr. (Westport: Greenwood Publishers Group, 1981), p. 206.

[5] William F. Holmes, "Whitecapping: Anti-Semitism in the Populist Era," *American Jewish Historical Quarterly*, Vol. LXIII (March, 1974), p. 224.

Preface

Although the role of the Jews in the South, generally, has been recognized by historians, not much attention has been given to the role played by the Jews in Mississippi history. Historian Allen Nevins reported to the Conference on the Writing of Regional History in the south in 1965: "Nobody who knows Southern history needs to be told that from the earliest colonial days Jewish families of intellect, culture, and character enriched the life of the section. Particularly in the cities—Charleston, Savannah, Mobile, New Orleans, Memphis—did their piety, their enterprise, their zeal for education and the arts, and their philanthropy weave happy strands into the texture of Southern civilization." What Nevins says about Jewish communities in other parts of the South is also applicable to Mississippi cities such as Natchez, Vicksburg, Meridian, and Greenville.

A major reason why scholars have not given even closer attention to Jewish settlement and growth in the South is supplied by Leonard Dinnerstein and Mary Dale Palsson in their book *Jews in the South* and their explanation, of course, also applies to Mississippi's Jews. "They have usually drawn thoughtful analysis only during times of crisis when they became objects of prejudice and scorn. Except for different religious practices, Jews made every effort to become absorbed into the activities of their adopted home. Their life-style closely resembled that of their gentile neighbors, and this is one reason they have failed to attract the attention of historians interested in the uniqueness of minority groups."

Who were the Jews who came to Mississippi, bringing energy for building and sustaining new towns in a new world? When we asked this question in a public request for information in Jewish regional and national Jewish newspapers the response was full and enthusiastic. People from all over the state and beyond sent letters, photographs, and memorabilia. Their response, our visits to many parts of the state, our interviews with descendants, and our research yielded a remarkable collection of personal histories, illustrated by vintage photographs from family albums and scrapbooks.

We are particularly grateful to have had the following works that served as a foundation upon which we were able to build: *Inventory of the Church and Synagogue Archives of Mississippi, Jewish Congregations and Organizations*. Work Projects Administration, 1940; *American Jewish Landmarks* by Bernard Postal and Lionel Koppman; and *Memoirs of American Jews* by Jacob R. Marcus. Another volume, not specifically on Jewish aspects, was helpful in our search, namely, *Hometown Mississippi*, by James F. Brieger. Four mimeographed items contained invaluable histories of specific Jewish communities: *Greenville*, by Herbert W. Solomon; *Vicksburg*, by Gertrude

Phillipsborn; and *Natchez,* by Rabbi and Mrs. Julius Kerman, and one by an anonymous "bw."

In the course of the five-year-long project, we encountered the usual problems of historians. Historic records had been lost to fire, flood, or disregard. Sometimes the only indication of a Jewish population in a town was found in its cemetery. General population shifts whether caused by the ravages of the boll weevil, tornadoes, or yellow fever, naturally affected the Jews. Towns flourishing on river traffic dwindled when the river shifted its course or the railroad became the more important means of transportation. Although frequently it was the Jews who made for the healthy economy, because of the nature of their livelihood, these factors forced them to move in search of a substantial clientele.

The material collected here may not constitute a comprehensive gathering but it is a representative selection from over a thousand photographs and accompanying stories. It is a collection necessarily concentrated on the years since the advent of photography in the 1840s up into the early twentieth century. Although the scholarly approach was a primary concern in the making of this book, in-depth study, however, was not always a possibility. These photographs, nevertheless, are chroniclers on their own, creating impressions and making certain conclusions inescapable.

The remarkable stories here constitute a substantial addition to the documentation of the life of the Jewish people in the state; the faces and scenes shown in these old photographs offer, we believe, strong insight into a largely neglected part of Mississippi and American Jewish history.

Introduction

The photographs in this volume date from the 1840s (the early days of photography) to 1900. There is considerable evidence, however, that Jews were living in Mississippi long before the mid-nineteenth-century. In *American Jewish Landmarks*, Bernard Postal and Lionel Koppman report that a small number of French Jews may have come to Mississippi as early as 1699. When John Law, the famous adventurer and speculator, established the "Mississippi Company" to promote the settlement of the lower Mississippi valley in 1717, he deported a small group of "undesirables" from France to the Louisiana Province. Among those undesirables were a "certain number of people of standing," and it is possible that some of them were Jews. Many of them died because of the hardships they faced in that frontier country. "Among the surviving colonists," according to Postal and Koppman, "were two with familiar Jewish names, Simon Kuhn and Zweig."

In 1724 Governor Jean Baptiste LeMoyne, Sieur d' Bienville issued the Black Code. That body of laws contained a provision restricting further Jewish immigration to the Louisiana Province. Such restrictions indicate that some Jews were already in the Province. Under British rule, 1763–1783, this restriction was not enforced. Jews, however, were not allowed to exercise the right of franchise, which is still further evidence of the presence of Jews.

Bertram W. Korn, in *The Early Jews of New Orleans*, indicates that one of the Monsanto brothers of New Orleans lived for a time with his wife, Clara, in Natchez. Korn writes: "In 1785 . . . [Benjamin Monsanto] decided to undertake a planter's life in Natchez. He had no difficulty in becoming accepted as a member of the Natchez community; his knowledge of French, Spanish, and English meant that he was equally at home with all of the settlers in the area . . . Governor Manuel Gayoso de Lemos twice appointed him to teams of citizens who conducted inventories and appraisals of the estates of deceased neighbors, and in 1790 he was one of the men on a panel from whom arbitrators were chosen to compromise a dispute."

There is an interesting reference to the Monsantos in *American Jewish Landmarks*. Major Samuel S. Foreman of New Jersey, who visited Natchez in 1789, later sent a report to the Department of War. In his report, Major Foreman wrote that "in the village of Natchez there resided Monsier [sic] and Madam [sic] Mansante—Spanish Jews, I think, who were the most kind and hospitable of people."

Landmarks also includes references to two other early Jewish settlers. The first was Charles Lewis Levin, an eccentric school teacher from South Carolina who came to Mississippi in 1828 to teach at Woodville. Levin was badly wounded in a duel in which his second was Jefferson

Davis, later president of the Confederacy. The other settler was Dr. Joseph Hertz, who practiced medicine at Natchez in 1835.

Another valuable source which provides information about early Jewish settlers in Mississippi is a typewritten paper written by a modest "bw" of Natchez whose identity we were not able to ascertain. Evidently, "bw" and a Mrs. Frank, and "three investigators [who] have passed to the great beyond" were collaborators in his research. Their findings were to be published in a monthly journal of some sort. From internal evidence, it is assumed that this document was written around 1950. The primary sources that the investigators consulted were court records. Mention is made of quite a few Jewish-sounding names in the years 1783, 1788, 1794, and 1838. Some of the persons mentioned in the document may have been Jews, but some probably were not. The paper mentions a tombstone in the Natchez cemetery, bearing the name of Harris and the date 1828. It also mentions several other people by the name of Harris. We had the good fortune to stumble upon some old cemetery records that proved to be very helpful. In the early 1820s, when two Jewish peddlers died in Natchez, a Jew by the name of Harris purchased a plot for their burial in the city cemetery. A retired caretaker took us to the spot and explained that that portion of the cemetery had washed away long ago into the bayou down below. The records also identified Harris as a Jew, and we were able to locate his gravestone, which bore the date of 1828. Harris's grave stands at the edge of the old Catholic portion of the city cemetery.

Background for Migration

In the middle of the eighteenth century, Jews were scattered throughout many parts of the world. It has been estimated that the total Jewish population at that time was only about three million. In central Europe Jews were concentrated in the principalities of Bohemia, Bavaria, Moravia, and Alsace-Lorraine, and in large cities such as Berlin, Hamburg, and Frankfurt am Main.

Most European nations were divided into a small privileged class on the one hand and the unprivileged masses on the other. Under these conditions Jews occupied a status even lower than second class. Thus, when the French Revolution occurred in 1789, the condition of Jews could only get better. Even under Napoleon, with his vast conquests, Jews benefitted greatly. They became citizens of European states and provinces, with poltiical and economic rights, for the first time in a thousand years.

Progress, however, is not always measured along a continuum running steadily upwards; progress is more often intermittent. People tire quickly of revolution and reform. With the fall of Napoleon, a vast European reaction took place. Prince Von Metternich of Austria, a new force in Europe, was wary of change. After Napoleon's defeat at Waterloo in 1815 a prolonged war was waged against the enlightenment and liberalism the French Revolution had fostered. Wherever this war was successful, Jews, along with the masses in general, suffered a host of restrictions. They were segregated into ghettoes; special taxes were imposed upon them; their trade and travel was restricted; and even the number of Jewish marriages was regulated.

Jews could no longer live safely in their European homes. So they sought haven and opportunity in the United States, a country that had translated the theories on which its revolution was based into established rights for all its citizens. Emigration, however, meant leaving a fatherland of many centuries, the old synagogue where faith was kept alive, the old cemetery where family of several generations lay buried, and parents, brothers and sisters. Nevertheless, in 1815 Jewish people seeking a new life in a new world began a modern exodus from many German principalities.

Louis Zara wrote about Jews of colonial America; yet his words apply as well to the German Jews of the nineteenth century:

The primary motive that inspired, indeed often compelled, Jews to leave their homelands and pioneer in the New World was the quest for fuller freedom, freedom to worship, freedom to trade, and freedom to strive for that measure of human equality so generally denied to them even in the most hospitable of Old World lands. . . . Those who ventured forth to pit themselves against perils unknown were, naturally, of the sturdiest fiber. In many an instance, the only 'risk capital' they possessed was dear life itself.

Yet they came not as nomads on the wind, but as members of a group that had a sound religious faith to sustain them through the bitterest days. With them, they carried also a rare moral courage and cultural values not to be despised even in areas where the wilderness still loomed threateningly over scrawny settlements.

"The Southern Story,"
Anti-Defamation League Bulletin, June 1958, p. 1

Jewish immigration to America peaked in 1848 but continued for several years thereafter. Thousands of Jews came in waves, and it has been estimated that approximately 250,000 German Jews had come to this country by 1890.

Most of the Jews who immigrated to Mississippi from German-speaking lands during the 1840–1860 period came in sailing vessels which took up to sixty days to make the journey from Europe to New Orleans. The trip from New Orleans up the Mississippi River to Vicksburg took another six days. Those who came to Mississippi during this early period did not have the help of the immigrant aid societies which later proved to be of such value to Jewish immigrants to the Atlantic states in the 1880s. These aid societies were not established until well after the Civil War. The German Jews of previous migrations, however, came to the aid of each successive wave of new arrivals.

Why One and Not the Other?

There were thousands of other immigrants who came to America during this same period and in northern states large ethnic enclaves from various European countries were established. Although there were some ethnic groups in Mississippi, the number of these various groups was not large enough to make them highly visible. On the other hand, even though the Jewish population was not very large it was large enough to be highly visible.

European craftsmen and laborers did not come to the South because they knew that they would have to compete with slave labor. The Jews came to the South, however, because they were imbued with the spirit of the entrepreneur and, since they were deprived of the possibility of land ownership in the country from which they emigrated, they had an increasing desire to own land. There was opportunity in Mississippi where land was cheap.

The Land of Promise

The intoxicating scent of liberty wafted its way over the Atlantic and permeated the ghettoes and homes of the oppressed and the restless. News had come of opportunity and tolerance in the New World. It had come by word of mouth, by letters, and by reports in the Jewish press. America was a place where one could rise on merit rather than on the basis of favoritism within a group. It was a place where one could readily engage in business on one's own; and in slow, seemingly endless journeys in sailing vessesls, Jews streamed toward this shining example, the wonder of the ages, a true democracy!

Even though the country was going through a cycle of high and low economic periods during the early nineteenth century, the American economy on the whole was growing and expanding. Hence, it was an advantageous time for Jews not only from German-speaking lands but also from Russia and Poland to come and settle here.

America was built by the young and the willing. But in this volatile and dynamic country prejudice lingered among the various ethnic groups, especially in the principal cities of the Northeast. Thus, many Jews settled in the West and in the South, including Mississippi.

Adjustments to Be Made

Transplantation, of course, must have been a painful process. Some of the pain was eased, however, when relatives or friends had already established roots here. With their help and guidance, the newcomer was able to make adjustments through a difficult time.

When Jews came to Mississippi, more often than not, they started out without any capital. They had to give up their Yiddish or German for English. They came into a way of life marked by the plantation and an economy based largely on cotton and slavery. It did not, however, take them long to adjust to their new life-style, to Southern customs and business practices. For example, Louis Schmier explained in *Reflections of Southern Jewry* the necessity for the Jewish shopkeeper to keep his place of business open on Saturday, the Jewish Sabbath. The Jewish Sunday School was established because of "the need to acculturate the outward trappings of the educational process utilized by the Jewish community to the model set by the surrounding Christian churches."

The Americanization Process

When Jews came to Mississippi from European countries they understood well that they were no longer compelled to live in ghettoes. No government decrees would make special distinctions between them and their fellow citizens. They felt free to become as American as were their fellow Americans.

Beginnings, however, are sometimes difficult, and there were those who, although they cherished the language of their newly-adopted country, were reluctant to yield the German of their former homes. Early prayerbooks retained some German translations of the Hebrew. In Greenville, for example, the first rabbi to serve the Jewish community conducted a German-English school. The school building later became the town's first synagogue.

Some immigrants felt that the German *Kultur* was superior to the frontier life which they encountered here. Jewish leaders, however, sought to have their people understand that to become American they must "talk American" and most Jewish immigrants showed their eagerness to adjust by learning English as soon as possible. Peddlers and businessmen readily conducted their business affairs in the new language. Children in school learned it quickly and brought it home to teach to their parents.

The Americanization of Jewish immigrants was sometimes evident in the anglicization of their names. The Dreifus family of Meridian, for example, translated the German literally into Threefoot. Many families continued, however, to maintain their Jewish identity. Jacob R. Marcus, in *Memoirs*, cites another similar situation.

"Down in Natchez, Jacob Mayer finally became

John Mayer, but the customs and practices of Judaism were not forgotten at home. His older children bore European-influenced names like Emma, Simon, and Theresa, but his youngest son, born in 1864, in the midst of the war, was called [after a favorite Confederate officer] Joseph Eggleston Johnston Mayer."

In a free society the Jew could contrive to assimilate, i.e., shed his Jewish identity entirely and be as American or even more American than his neighbors. He could, also, in the spirit of his newly-adopted country, become a full citizen and yet maintain his dignity as a self-respecting Jew. So Jewish leaders taught that people could be good Americans without compromising their Jewish loyalties.

Wherever the authors wandered in Mississippi, they found that Jews had built their synagogues with great pride and learned with great satisfaction that the structures were regarded by the general population with great approval.

The authors have also found through the first three generations and even into the fourth that very few Jews married outside the Jewish community. But there was much visiting back and forth among young Jews, male and female, with friends in Jewish communities in neighboring towns within Mississippi as well as in the surrounding states of Alabama, Louisiana, and Tennessee. A study of the marriage records kept by Rabbi Seymour G. Bottigheimer of Natchez, with rare exception, indicates this quite clearly.

Even so, there was much social interaction between Jew and non-Jew, for it was the feeling of the Christian that the enlightenment of American life allowed for differences. As for the Jew, it was his feeling that this was America, where neighborliness was a natural thing. Both the frontier and the small towns fostered the feeling that the former alien need not be alienated.

The Jew and His Religion

The Jew's religion was also subject to the Americanization process. When he was confined to the ghetto, he had almost no choice with regard to adherence to his faith. In European countries the Jewish communities were autonomous and their leaders were responsible to the monarch. Hence, some Jews were compelled by government arrangement to be a Jew, at least outwardly. The Jew who might otherwise deny Jewish orthodoxy was constrained by public opinion within the ghetto to make manifest his Jewish loyalties.

When Jews, however, came to this country with its freedoms and opportunities they had several options. They could retain the Old World Judaism or modify it in the spirit of American liberalism. Jews could have gotten lost within the ethnic melting pot. Since they had no distinguishing racial characteristics, they could have been easily assimilated into the American populace.

What happened then to the Jew and his religion in the villages and towns of Mississippi during the nineteenth century? The early immigrants found it necessary to establish the beginnings of a Jewish cemetery. When enough Jews had gathered at a central point, they established a congregation. Sometimes they gathered in a home and sometimes they rented a room over a store for purposes of worship. Then the next step was to consider the building of a synagogue.

Frequently, orthodox Judaism was at first the pattern of worship. Yet the New World allowed for flexibility; modifications of the service were permitted and the use of the new prayerbook, called significantly, *Minhag America*, the American rite, was common. The Sunday School, an American institution, was adopted as a means of teaching children. The Natchez congregation was the first one in Mississippi to send two delegates to a convention held in 1873 in Cincinnati to form the Union of American Hebrew Congregations (Reform) and to institute a seminary for the training of rabbis for the American scene.

The Peddler

Many successful Jewish businesses in Mississippi can trace their history back to the energy enterprise of a single peddler. Peddling was often the way of life for many Jews in early Mississippi. It was a phenomenon in itself. A typical young Jewish man in his late teens or early twenties, having made his way across the Atlantic and through the Port of New Orleans, would arrive at a Mississippi town and oftimes find a friend or a relative who had already gone through the ped-

dler stage and was the owner of a store. The established merchant would give the newcomer the necessary pointers and would supply him, on easy credit terms, with an assortment of goods.

In most cases, the incipient entrepreneur carried his merchandise in a backpack, weighing about seventy-five pounds. Others were luckier and were able to begin by traveling on horseback. A few would ply the river towns and villages in a simple boat. Some started with a partner, but most began alone. Before venturing, however, all of them had to pick up some words and phrases in English, certainly the names of all the items they were to sell. They braved all kinds of terrain including the forests, rivers, and hills of the state. The forests were filled with many wild creatures. The young peddler could look upon some of them with wonder and delight: the deer, wild duck, geese, and quail, rabbits and squirrels. Then there were those to be feared: the bear, snakes, and wild dogs.

Stories of peddlers in northern states indicate that their experiences were not always pleasant. For the most part, peddlers in the South had easier and more pleasant experiences. Even so, one can well imagine what a frightening experience it must have been going through strange territory and approaching potential customers hardly knowing their language. In some situations, plantations and farms were several miles apart.

Usually, farmers and planters were kind to travellers, especially to peddlers who not only brought their wares but also brought news which was always at a premium on the remote plantations. They were invited into the home for a drink of water and were welcomed to stay for a meal or two and were often provided lodging for a night. If the peddler traveled on horseback, he was provided with food for his horse. There was usually a small charge for the meals and the lodging, but people would usually buy something because they had need of items in the peddler's pack. At other times they might make a purchase simply out of kindness. The slaves were also summoned and allowed to make purchases. Some peddlers would invariably leave a little item gratis for the children and for the lady of the house.

The peddler was also welcomed for reasons that had nothing to do with business. The number of blacks was dominant in rural Mississippi and so the farmers were always glad to see other whites. The blacks, too, were glad to see the stranger who, at first, was still wearing his European garb. Sometimes a peddler was invited to tell about life in his former European home and about travel across the Atlantic. If the peddler was a man of refinement—and frequently he was—he was able to bring a little culture to the frontier families upon whom he called.

Each peddler, of course, had his own experiences to recount to fellow peddlers when he returned after his period of travel of several weeks. One such experience is told by Julius Weis in *Memoirs:*

> . . . for a few days I happened to strike a very poor piece of country, about Brandywine Spring, Copiah Country, Miss. This country was settled mostly by poor white farmers, with very few negroes. My sales were very small, and I got very much discouraged. As the country was entirely strange to me, one day I had to do without my dinner, as I did not happen to get to a house at dinner time (noon). Shortly after noon, I came upon a negro who was on his way to Port Gibson with a load of cotton, and who had stopped beside the road to feed his oxen and eat his dinner. I went to him and asked him to give me a piece of his cornbread and a piece of meat, which he did, and I ate it with a great deal of relish, giving him a cotton handkerchief in payment. The next day I started out in a different direction, and met with much better success.

Many Southern peddlers were able not only to make a living from peddling but also to accumulate enough capital to go into business and eventually send for their families left behind in Europe. They were able to do this because the plantation owners were, as a general rule, more affluent than Northern farmers. Thus more Southern peddlers were able to ascend the ladder of success than their Northern counterparts. The peddling experience of most Mississippi Jews was a transitional step in becoming a successful and established merchant.

An interesting sidelight on the peddler's success story may be found in some statistics on that "new gadget," the telephone. The city directory of Meridian reports that in the year 1882 there were fifty telephone exchange listings. Although the Jews constituted a small proportion of the population, nine of those listings were of highly successful Jewish business firms.

Occupations

Mississippi Jews engaged in practically every field of business and entered virtually every vocation and profession. Only in America was such vocational freedom of choice open to Jews. The authors' findings show that Mississippi Jews were engaged in the following businesses and professions:

bankers	saddle makers
doctors	liquor sales
dentists	scrap metals
lawyers	hides, wool, furs
grocers	inns and hotels
confections	tobacco sales
mule sales	ice manufacture
rabbis	cotton farming
jewelers	restaurants
feeds	cotton brokers
bakers	butchers
laundry	furniture sales
saddle makers	leather goods
newspaper publishers	accountants
cotton compress	pawn shop
book sellers	merchants, clothes
plantation supplies	school teachers
liverystables	shoe manufacture
department stores	newspaper editor
farm implements	

One incentive for Jews to become involved in agriculture, landowning, growing cotton, and buying and selling cotton, was that in most European countries they had not been permitted to own land, which, of course, was possible in Mississippi.

Education and Culture

One can only venture to guess about the education and culture of the Jews of Mississippi in the period this book covers but a few examples might be of some help. Almost all Jewish children went to schools for elementary and secondary education. In Greenville, five out of thirteen of the first graduating class of the high school were Jews. There were families who sent their children to well-known schools in the East, such as Andover and Yale.

In Meridian, the Jewish owners of a large department store sponsored and managed the Grand Opera House, which brought famous talent from the East to its stage. The first presentation was Strauss's "The Gypsy Baron." One of the many guest artists who appeared at the Opera House was the celebrated operatic tenor Enrico Caruso. The administrators of the Opera House were, we were told, satisfied "to break even."

What Allan Nevins said about colonial "Jewish families of intellect, culture and character" enriching their environment seems applicable in the case of many Jewish families of Mississippi. These impressions are strengthened by A. L. Sachar's comment, in *A History of the Jews*, concerning the German Jews in general:

> The German settlers . . . were able, intelligent, and willing to learn in a land of unique opportunity. Their children were given every advantage and many of them rose to distinguished leadership in Jewish and American life.

Civic Activity

Judge Jeff Truly of Natchez reminisced in a letter written to Clara Eiseman Scharff on the occasion of her eightieth birthday. He wrote about the "great good which the Jewish merchants did to the towns of Natchez, Fayette, Rodney, Union Church, and Port Gibson, before, after, and during the Confederate War and throughout the . . . days of . . . Reconstruction."

Jews, once they became established in homes and businesses, became active in town, city, county and state affairs. In the period covered by this book there were at least seven Jewish mayors, five councilmen or aldermen, a city treasurer, two tax collectors, four school board trustees, one county supervisor, and at least two representatives in the state legislature. One of the most active Jewish politicians was Cassius L. Tillman of Natchez who held many different political offices.

Many Jews held high office in the Masonic order, the Knights of Pythias, and in the Odd Fellows organization. Charles Blum of Nitta Yuma served a term as the master of the state organization of Masons. Mrs. Ricka Tillman of Natchez was on the board of the Protestant Orphans

Home. In Meridian and in Brookhaven the chiefs of the fire department were Jews.

Jew and Gentile

Morris U. Schappes, in *A Documentary History of the Jews in the United States, 1654–1875*, explains how Jewish and non-Jewish settlers accommodated each other:

> Although settlers [non-Jewish] retained their Old World prejudices, most of them realized the need for a diversified economy, and they welcomed the special talents and skills attributed to the Jews. In the North as well as in the South, many Jews prospered, especially as artisans, financiers, and merchants. The ghetto, a product of European feudalism, existed nowhere in this country.

In early times in Mississippi history, Jews and Christians found themselves in the same boat, so to speak, and understood that, if progress was to be made in their young communities, all members must help with the rowing. This attitude emerged especially during the Civil War, when both Christian and Jewish Mississippians found themselves fighting for the same cause. The same applied during the period of Reconstruction. Beyond all this, there must also have been a general feeling of neighborliness.

Investigation in this matter would tend to indicate a high level of social interaction between Jews and Christians. This conclusion is the result of inquiries in various communities. It also comes from a variety of items in various publications.

It is true, of course, that one cannot arrive at scientific conclusions on the basis of a few examples taken over a period of several decades. Nevertheless, these examples merit full consideration. No doubt, communities within the same state may differ greatly in character. But what Dave Rattray, author of *The City of Natchez*, wrote about Natchez in 1881 could well apply to other Mississippi communities:

> English, Irish, Scotch, Italians, a few French and Germans, of origin and nativity, and an excellent class of Hebrews, make up the population. Between the latter and the Christians, the social line is less distinct than in any part of the Union, and Jews and Gentiles freely intermingle in every enterprise of commerce, charity or public advancement.

When Jewish communities were in their infancy and had not yet built their synagogues, it was quite common for a church to allow their facilities for a Jewish wedding. The newspaper eulogies of those days spoke frequently of businesses closing during the funeral of a prominent Jew in respect for the Jewish dead. It seems that in small towns anyone's loss was everyone's loss.

In early Brookhaven, E. H. Wentworth, a prominent citizen, large property-holder, and a non-Jew, donated the land for the Jewish cemetery.

In 1884, Greenville Jews held an observance marking the hundredth birthday anniversary of Sir Moses Montefiore, a British benefactor of Jewish causes. A Methodist minister, the Reverend M. Standifer, pronounced the benediction at the ceremony.

When young Jewish communities needed funds to build a new temple, they sometimes sponsored a "benefit affair" for the general public, who participated whole-heartedly and generously. A good example of this is described in the *Natchez Weekly Democrat* of October 26, 1870:

> We learn that our Israelite fellow citizens are making extensive preparations for a fair to be held on the 1st of November next for the purpose of raising funds to complete their handsome synagogue. Synagogue which is an ornament to our city.
>
> The enterprising ladies and gentlemen engaged in this good work, give an earnest of success. Contributions are solicited, which can be left at the store of Mr. Simon Mayer or with Mrs. John Mayer.

On November 17, 1870, the same paper printed this "Card of Thanks":

> The ladies of the Hebrew Aid Association take much pleasure in informing the public that they realized the sum of $2,509.10, net proceeds of the Fair lately given by them in this city. They would in this manner return their sincere thanks to their friends here and abroad for the liberal patronage and donations. . . .
>
> Mrs. John Mayer, President

Non-Jewish musicians would often play the organ, the violin, and sing in the choir for special occasions. In Natchez, Mr. Van Nordragen was hired to instruct and lead the choir. In 1905, Mr. Ferris Bradley was engaged by the Natchez temple as organist and served in that capacity for fifty years.

In Meridian, the St. Paul's Episcopal group was organized in 1901. Before the congregation built its own building, the first service and confirmation were held in the Meridian synagogue. Later, when the Meridian temple suffered a serious fire in 1907, the people of St. Paul's offered their building for Jewish services during the time when the temple was being repaired. The time came later when the Episcopal church was being remodeled and the congregation again made use of Temple Beth Israel.

When the Natchez temple burned in 1903, Christians sent donations to the rebuilding fund and three different church groups—Methodist, Baptist, and Episcopal—offered the free use of their buildings. The congregation accepted the first offer, which was made by the Jefferson Street Methodist Church. The Jewish congregation subsequently sent a gift of $200 to the church as a token of its appreciation.

When the new temple in Greenville was being built in 1905–1906, holy day services were held in the First Christian Church.

The Summit Sun reported in its April 4, 1940, anniversary edition: "When the late Isadore Moyse, pioneer Jewish citizen of Summit died a wash-out on the railroad made it impossible for the family to secure the services of a rabbi and Dr. Otken, the local Baptist minister, was requested to officiate at his funeral services. He did so, choosing his text from the Old Testament."

A clipping from the Lexington newspaper reports on the fiftieth anniversary service of the temple in Lexington: "Mayor Allie Povall expressed the sentiments of the entire community when he said during Sunday's program: 'The Jewish people of Lexington have been good citizens and glad to assume their full share of the duties of citizenship. Their interest and participation in the various activities of community life has been outstanding. . . . I feel sure that every family in Lexington who has been in sorrow or sickness has at some time known kindnesses extended by members of this congregation.'"

A note should be included here with regard to the Jewish community's relationship with black

Mississippians. Very little information was found on this subject during the research for this book. John Dollard, however, made a study of group interrelationships in Indianola for his book, *Caste and Class in a Southern Town* (1937), and his brief comment provides some insight into the matter. Dollard explains the success of Jewish merchants in the Delta by saying that "the Jews have treated negroes with courtesy, or at least without discourtesy, in strictly business relations" and that the Jews "bargain with the negroes and the negroes like this. . . . Southern whites tend to be brusque and 'take-it' or 'leave-it' with the negro, while Jews are more considerate, putting business before caste."

The Shadow Side

As cordial and cooperative as the relationship between Jews and non-Jews normally was during most of the early nineteenth century, there were problems at times which the honest historian must report. One particular incident, for which Mississippians were not directly responsible, took place at Holly Springs in the northern part of the state. General Ulysses S. Grant issued his infamous Order No. 11 in 1862, which expelled all Jews from the war zone known as the Department of Tennessee, which included the state of Mississippi. Northerners had come down to trade in Southern cotton. There was much dealing in contraband, and this made for chaos and corruption. There may have been some Jews involved, but if there were, they were a very small portion of those involved, certainly not enough to condemn an entire people. Someone, however, had to be blamed. A delegation of Jews from Kentucky went to Washington to appeal to President Abraham Lincoln, who, understanding what was involved, forthwith countermanded the order.

It has already been indicated that Jews and Christians got along well during the Civil War. Nevertheless, it is necessary to tell about Henry S. Foote, who was a Mississippi governor, United States Senator and Confederate Congressman. *Landmarks* describes Foote's attack on Jews as follows:

> Foote, a member of the Confederate Congress during Civil War, waged a violent campaign of anti-semitism. He denounced Judah P. Benjamin (a Jew), Secretary of War and Secretary of State of the Confederate States . . . for allegedly protecting 'Jewish profiteers who dominated the United States and who would own everything after the war.

Despite Foote's dire prediction, Jews and Christians labored side by side courageously during the turmoil of the Reconstruction period. *Landmarks* also reports, however, the formation of the "White Caps," a movement directed against blacks and Jews during the agricultural depression of the 1890s and early 1900s. This activity was detailed by William F. Holmes in the *American Jewish Historical Quarterly*.

One Jew in the southern part of the state inspired anti-Jewish feeling and probably deserved it because of the many mortgage foreclosures which he mercilessly executed. The actions of the White Caps forced him to move to New Orleans. Fortunately, the citizens of his community understood this to be an isolated incident.

The Civil War

One of the most interesting aspects of American Jewish history is the fact that the Civil War divided the Jewish community in the same way it divided the country at large. Although the Jewish population was comparatively small, several thousand Jewish soldiers fought with zeal on both sides in the War-Between-the-States. "Jewish Johnny Reb," to borrow a colorful expression from Jacob R. Marcus, fought "Jewish Billy Yank" on the battlefield. Mississippi Jews played a significant role as soldiers, in this case, of course, on behalf of the Confederate cause. There were privates and officers in both the infantry and cavalry.

It is wise to remember here what Jacob R. Marcus says in his *Memoirs*: [What we say about the Southern Jew] "must not obscure the fact that he was a regional type, for frequently, though not always, he was a Southern particularist, and only secondly a citizen of the United States. After all, he could not escape his environment; the pattern he followed was the pattern of a host of Southerners."

It is challenging to speculate why Jews from similar backgrounds would espouse two diametrically opposed causes. It is understandable that the Northern Jew fought for freedom and the abolition of slavery. After all, one of the most important of Jewish holy days is Passover, the festival of freedom, which commemorates the emancipation of the Hebrews from slavery under the Egyptian pharaoh. Furthermore, the preamble to the Ten Commandments states explicitly [Exodus 20:2]: "I am the Lord thy God who brought thee out of the land of Egypt, out of the house of bondage." Here God's principal role is that of Emancipator. Then, too, the Jew knew well from his history what oppression meant. In fact, the reason for his coming to America was the lack of civil rights in the Old World.

What sociological phenomena would lead the Southern Jew to fight so fervently for the principle of slavery? Why was he willing to sacrifice his life so readily for a cause that he knew was contrary to religious principle? In their former European lands of oppression Jews actually sought to avoid conscription by any means; yet here in the South they fought willingly and with zest.

Did the Jew's support for the Confederacy stem from gratitude to that part of his newly-adopted country that supplied him with such valuable rights and privileges and improved his living status? Was it that he was afraid to show his neighbor his real feelings? Life often calls for compromises. Did the good life make it easy to forget the hardships of his fellow human beings? War brings its own fervor and it stirs an intense patriotism. Was the Jew caught up by the flag-waving and the clamor for states' rights he beheld in his fellow citizens? Was the hysteria of his fellow citizens infectious and did it seize him in the same way? Whatever the answer, the heartache of it all is revealed in the following letter of Julius Yaretzky, of Shuqualak, to his son:

Dear Frank,
You wish to know about what I, if any, had left and brought home with me from the War, such as arms or otherwise. So I will inform you fully of it.

I did not bring anything home with me for the following good reasons. When I was in the army, I possessed a large knife, pistol and sword. The knife I found useless in battle and left it at Pensacola, Fla. Navy Yard, as we evacuated that place to go to Corinth, Miss. to participate in the battle of Shiloh

or Farmington called by same. The pistol was a Colts powder & ball and it was damaged in the battle of Perriville, Ky. and became useless. The cilinder (sic) of same was struck by a ball from grape shot and, therefore, (I) did not have any further use for it. The sword was taken from me when I was captured at the Battle of Franklin, Tenn. near Nashville. I tried to get the Yanks to let me keep it so I could bring it home but was refused and was compelled to give it up. So, dear boy, I have none of the war relics left to send you but a good record of a faithful soldier I then was.

I was taken prisoner and sent to Johnson's Island, Ohio, on Lake Erie near Sandusky, Ohio. I was, with others, held as prisoner of war until the Confederate army surrendered. Then we all were sent home.

I went from there to New York and thence to Alexandria, Va. where General Grant's and Sherman's armies were mustered out of service. I then came south. I would like to read one of those books (about the war). What can one be bought for and where are they published?

I was also in several other Battles such as Atlanta, Ga.; Marietta, Ga.; Chickamoga (sic); and some other small ones. But, thanks to our Heavenly Father, He brought me safe through all.

I do not advise any one to go to war, for it is a hard life, more so when you engage in it for pay only. The war between the states was for principles of states' rights, but the South lost and we of the South think as well of the Brother in North now as well as when we did before the war. Hoping you are in good health. Write often. . . .

Your father

(Courtesy: Mrs. Joyce Siegel, Baton Rouge, Louisiana)

Reconstruction, 1865–1876

The Brookhaven Centennial Historical Program, 1859–1959, described the many postwar problems and credited the town's Jewish citizens for their contributions to rebuilding the town after the war:

The men . . . surrendered all ordinance equipment. They were then sent home where relatives, hungry and fearful, welcomed them. Together once more with families, friends, and the soldiers of other mustered-out companies, they awaited the beginning of an unhappy, intolerant era.

As these men doffed their uniforms and reverently laid away the flags of the Confederacy, they must have had to muster more of the courage spoken of so glowingly by General French. Their future was anything but bright; the town with its empty, bankrupt stores clustered around a deserted railroad station; the college closed, it campus serving as a cemetery for Southern soldiers; the fine homes delapidated with most of the glory gone; the livestock stolen or starved; Confederate money useless; their rights as citizens in jeopardy—no, not a happy prospect for the future.

But we need to remember that many of these men were Brookhaven's first citizens. They had helped to build their town from nothing once. They swiftly squared their shoulders and set out to build it again.

. . . During these years men like . . . Cohn Abrams, George and Elias Bowsky . . . Maurice Dreyfus . . . Max and Josh Priebatsch . . . and many others came in to build businesses and become good citizens. The town began to grow and prosper.

Shoulders and Roots

We have become a nation concerned with our roots, probably because so many of us have become rootless. The comment of Rabbi Samuel E. Karff of Houston can have great significance for us: "Times change. Moods change. Needs change. We must respond accordingly . . . but . . . we are standing on the shoulders of those who came before us."

In their book, *The Lessons of History*, Will and Ariel Durant evaluate what they have learned from a lifetime of studying history:

No one man, however brilliant or well-informed, can come in one lifetime to such fullness of understanding as to safely judge and dismiss the customs and institutions of his society, for these are the wisdom of generations after centuries of experience in the laboratory of history. . . . Roots are more vital than grafts.

Jews in Early
Mississippi

Woodville

At one time Woodville enjoyed a very large Jewish population, with several of the town's leading and most respected merchants being of your faith. Our old files reveal the names of numerous Jewish families, some of whom I remember. Unfortunately, with the advent of the boll weevil our economy declined and a resultant exodus of Jews followed as attested to in our files of that period.

John S. Lewis, Editor
The Woodville Republican

JEWS played a substantial role in the development of communities in southwestern Mississippi. The town of Woodville, well-known for its newspaper the *Woodville Republican* (established 1824 and operated continuously since that time) and for Wilkinson Academy, which was attended by Jefferson Davis from nearby Rosemont, had a large and active Jewish community. The town was even called, affectionately, "Little Jerusalem."

Founded about 1809, Woodville picked up momentum in its growth when the West Feliciana Railroad came in 1831. Its prosperity attracted Jewish businessmen to the town, and their activities added increased economic and cultural benefits to Woodville.

Jewish religious services began to be held in Woodville as early as 1850. In the late 1860s the Woodville Hebrew Educational Association was formed. Congregation Beth Israel (Hebrew: House of Israel) was the outgrowth of that organization, and the town's first synagogue was built in 1878. The building was destroyed by fire in 1896 and a cornerstone for a new temple was dedicated on that site in July of the same year.

The second synagogue, shown here, was, like the former building, of wooden construction. By 1910, there were no longer any Jews in Wood-

The town was even called, affectionately, "Little Jerusalem."

Courtesy *The Woodville Republican*

ville, and the building was used first as a school and then as a theatre. In the 1930s it was destroyed by fire.

Wilkinson County Jews, most of them from Woodville, enlisted to fight for the Confederacy from 1861 to 1865. Among them were Solomon Loeb, Company K16, Mississippi Regiment, Wilkinson Rifles; Joseph Kohn and F. Rosenberg, Company D, 38th Mississippi Regiment, Wilkinson Guards, Infantry; J. Cline and Henry Cline, Company E, 21st Mississippi Regiment, Hurricane Rifles, Infantry. Gus Kann also served in the infantry and Isaac T. Hart served in the Confederate Guard.

Jews from Woodville's early years are interred behind this fence, designed by Henderer's Iron Fence Works, New Orleans. According to *American Jewish Landmarks*, "the cemetery was conse-

crated in 1848 when two peddlers, Jacob Schwartz and Jacob Cohen paid $50 for a small plot to bury a fellow peddler, Henry Brugance."

Rabbi Emanuel M. Rosenfelder was born in Germany in 1843 and came to the United States in 1867. In February, 1873, he came to Woodville, where in 1874 he received his citizenship certificate.

A letter of reference, commendation, and severance from the Woodville Hebrew Educational Association, dated July 17, 1874, speaks of him affectionately as a rabbi, teacher, and reader, as well as an accomplished lecturer. Signed by Isaac T. Hart, president, the letter states Rabbi Rosenfelder's desire to visit Germany as the reason for severance. Fortified by his citizenship papers, he felt free to return to his native country for a visit.

Upon his return, he may have served as a circuit rider in Louisiana. He married a native New Orleanian in 1876, and they went to his new congregation in Natchez. In *Reflections of Southern Jewry*, Charles Wesselowsky writes of a visit to Natchez in 1878–1879 and of "Rev. Mr. Rosenfelder, whom we found to be an intelligent and polished scholar, well worth and deserving the function he occupies."

The *Natchez Daily Democrat* carried an article in 1880 that announced that the Reverend Dr. E. M. Rosenfelder resigned from Temple B'nai Israel after several years "owing to a defect in his eyesight" to take up residence in Louisville, Kentucky.

Gabe Kann (1843–1922) was born in Woodville. He served throughout the war, 1861–1865,

as bugler of Company K, 16th Mississippi Regiment. After the war, he married Julia Aaronstein of St. Francisville, Louisiana.

The old Gabe Kann building on the south side of Woodville's court square where he had his drug store, was razed in 1960. The business advertisement read: "G. Kann, Drugs, Medicines and Chemicals, Prescriptions carefully filled, day and night . . . patent medicines, fancy goods, sundries, perfumes . . . trusses . . . window glass, putty, paints, oils, varnishes, etc. etc."

Courtesy *The Woodville Republican*

Isaac T. Hart (1834–1905) was one of the most highly respected residents of Woodville, according to the Exposition edition of the *Woodville Republican*. The article went on to say, "He was born in Kingston, Jamaica . . . At the age of fourteen he came to New Orleans and secured a position as a clerk for Majors Beard, a real estate . . . dealer and, after his death, as a senior mem-

Courtesy *The Woodville Republican*

ber, he formed a partnership with the son, Dr. Beard."

In 1861, he enlisted in the Confederate Guard, Company B. After the war and a short stay in Mexico, Hart and his family moved to Woodville in 1864. His wife Josephine (Adolphus) Hart (1836–1929) was born in Trenton, New Jersey.

As president of Congregation Beth Israel, he was influential in bringing both Rabbi Emanuel Rosenfelder and Rabbi Henry Cohen to serve the congregation.

The newspaper article also states, "He has always been an active and ardent supporter of secret orders. He was the grand master of Mississippi in 1873 [of the] IOOF [Odd Fellows] [and was] worshipful master of Asylum Lodge, No. 63, ASIAM [?], Woodville, and I.O.B.B. [Independent Order of B'nai B'rith]."

Ellis T. Hart (1861–1926) was born in New Orleans, Louisiana, and was the son of Isaac and Josephine (Adolphus) Hart. He came to Woodville with his parents at age three in 1864.

His first mercantile ventures were in Centreville and Louisiana villages before going into business in Woodville.

Like his father, Ellis Hart was fond of secret societies, and he was a past grand master of the Odd Fellows of the state, a Mason, a Pythian, a member of the Legion of Honor, and of the Knights of Honor.

Courtesy *Henry Cohen, Messenger of the Lord*, Stanley A. Dreyfus, ed.

Courtesy *The Woodville Republican*

Ellis Hart

Rabbi Henry Cohen was born in 1863 in London where he received his education. When he was eighteen he traveled in Africa as an interpreter for a French legation. While there, he was severely wounded during the Zulu war when his party was attacked by the natives.

His first assignment as a rabbi was the congregation in Kingston in the British West Indies, which he served for only the one year, 1884–1885. His trip home to London was interrupted by a message from Isaac T. Hart saying that he was to be the rabbi of the congregation in Woodville, which he served for the years 1885 to 1888.

For its centennial edition in 1924, the *Woodville Republican* reported: "No minister who ever served a church in Woodville was more popular than was Rabbi Henry Cohen, who is now stationed at Galveston, Texas, but who still retains his love for Woodville."

Strict observance of the Jewish Sabbath on the seventh day of the week called for it to be a day of rest with services in the morning. Rabbi Cohen sought to adhere to this tradition at least in part when the men of his congregation pointed out that Saturday was an important day of business, especially when the farmers came into town. A happy compromise was reached. The

For its centennial edition in 1924, the Woodville Republican *reported: "No minister who ever served a church in Woodville was more popular than was Rabbi Henry Cohen."*

men consented to keep their stores closed in the morning for the duration of the service, which they attended faithfully mostly because they were fond of the young rabbi and enjoyed his engaging manner and skillful preaching.

Since the farmers were aware that the Jewish stores would be closed, most of them postponed their visit into town until the afternoon. Some, however, came in the morning to hear Rabbi Cohen preach. The non-Jewish merchants decided that they, too, might just as well close up shop for the morning and some of them also attended the service to hear the eloquent young preacher.

Charles Cohen (1860–1945) was born in Montgomery, Alabama, and came to Woodville as a child. He went daily from his home in Woodville to Ashwood, Mississippi, a railroad stop with a station three miles away. There he had a large mercantile business where he catered to the needs of train travelers and farmers in the area who would come to his establishment for general merchandise.

Cohen had large property holdings and was a director of the Bank of Woodville.

Abe Cohen Courtesy *The Woodville Republican*

ville. His first business experience was with his brother at the Ashwood store. In 1901, he embarked in business with A. Metzger to form Metzger & Cohen.

The Cohen Mercantile, located on the northwest side of the courthouse square, as it appeared shortly after the turn of the century. It was destroyed by fire in 1932

Charles Cohen   Courtesy *The Woodville Republican*

The younger brother of Charles Cohen was Abe Cohen (1871–1941) who was born in Wood-

Courtesy *The Woodville Republican*

Morris H. Rothchild was born in 1863 in Nordstetten, Germany, and migrated to America in 1880. He was employed in Woodville by P. Moller and Company, where his brother Martin (1856–1900) was a junior member.

Martin Rothchild bought out the interest of Moller and formed the company of Martin Rothchild and Brother. The general merchandise store prospered, and after Martin Rothchild died in 1900, Morris H. Rothchild bought out the interest of the heirs.

By 1904 Morris Rothchild's business became an extensive jobbing and retail enterprise in general merchandise. In addition, the cotton buying department handled a volume of about 8,000 bales in season.

Rothchild was president of the Bank of Woodville, director of the Woodville Oil Manufacturing Company, and served as secretary of the school board.

The pictures include one of Morris H. Rothchild, his general merchandise store, and the company warehouse and cotton yard.

A. H. Sandman (1851–1919) was born in Charlottesville, Virginia, and attended the University of Virginia. After working in Atlanta, he

came to Woodville in 1890. Sandman was a director of the Bank of Woodville. He had a working plantation and a saloon.

Leon Schwartz was born in Woodville in 1874, the son of Jacob Schwartz (1815–1894) who had

Courtesy *The Woodville Republican*

come to Woodville from Engenheim, Germany.

At age twenty-one, Leon Schwartz was elected to be a member of the Board of Aldermen and retained the position for many years. He served as city clerk for a short time.

In 1896, Schwartz formed a partnership with C. H. Neyland (a non-Jew) to establish Schwartz & Neyland, fancy groceries and general merchandise.

He married Bessie Cohen of Farmersville, Texas, in 1904.

A native of Woodville, Sidney Rothchild was the son of Martin Rothchild, who formed the firm Martin Rothchild and Brother. After Sidney Rothchild graduated from the University of New

Orleans, he joined the firm owned by his uncle, Morris H. Rothchild.

Lee C. Schloss (1863–1933) was born in Memphis, Tennessee. He came to Woodville as a very young man and was employed by Ralph Gunst [a Jew] and Company. He married Eva Goslinski, a local girl. In 1891 he became the sole owner and publisher of the *Woodville Courier*, which he maintained until 1893. The following seventeen years until 1910 he was in business with Morris H. Rothchild. When the latter retired, Lee C. Schloss gradually bought out not only his interest but also the interests of the other members of the family to form Schloss Company in 1923.

Lee Schloss served as president of the school board, as a member of the city council, and as city treasurer for many years. It was largely through the efforts of Schloss that Woodville gained an agricultural high school. During the days of the "separate but equal" period, a school for black students was built in Woodville with

money from the Rosenwald family of Philadelphia. It was named the Schloss-Rosenwald School. Photographs show Lee C. Schloss, his home, and Charles Murdock Schloss, the only child of Lee and Eva Schloss.

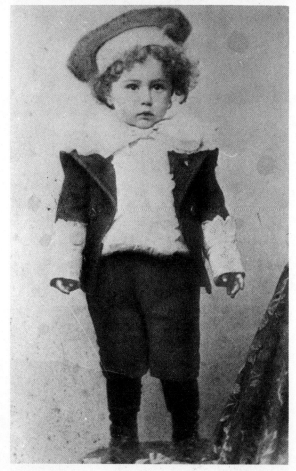

Photograph of the boy courtesy Charles M. Schloss, Jr., Englewood, Colorado

Natchez

DESPITE eighteenth century Spanish restrictions on voting rights, Jews began to filter into the Natchez area early. Some are said to have traded with Indian tribes in the vicinity.

The name of Benjamin Monsanto, whose wife Clara came from Curacao, appears on land records of the Natchez area in the 1790s. A lawsuit in Spanish legal records contains names that were possibly Jewish, like Israel Mayes or Mayer in 1783, Robert and F. Abrams in 1788. Pedro Siegle was listed as a witness in 1794.

A tombstone marked "A. Harris 1828" stands in the old Natchez cemetery and is identified in the margin of city cemetery records with the words "believed to be a Jew."

In 1817, as the Mississippi Territory moved toward statehood, the era of the Mississippi River steamboat began. Waves of immigrants moved into the new state in the 1840s and among the early arrivals were Jews from Germany and Alsace-Lorraine.

These early Jewish settlers frequently extended credit to later émigrés for merchandise they bought to begin life in Mississippi by peddling. Thus set up for business, the itinerant salesman would venture out into the countryside acquiring English "on the job." Eventually, peddlers strived to open stores in Natchez, which was a boom town.

Jewish business establishments, among others, were being built in the low-lying river region known as Natchez-Under-the-Hill. Their stores were crude, simple structures amid saloons and dance halls, all facing dirt streets. Ruffians, gamblers, riverboaters, and "ladies of ill repute," mingled with steamboat passengers and townspeople in the riverfront hubbub.

The steamboat later reigned on the river, and cotton was king on the land, making Natchez a great world port for cotton export. Natchez became an elegant city with stately mansions and magnificent plantations on its outskirts. Much of the cotton trade was done on credit in a place where a man's word was his bond. Duels of honor were fought frequently on a sand bar across the river.

Jewish shopkeepers John Mayer, Aaron Beekman, and David Moses, among other Jews of the 1840s, laid the true foundation of a robust Jewish community which thrived for more than a century.

Like their fellow Southerners, the Jews were loyal to the Confederacy. When the Union gunboat Essex *fired on Natchez, the only casualty was Rosalie, the seven-year-old daughter of Aaron and Fanny Beekman.*

Like their fellow Southerners, the Jews were loyal to the Confederacy. When the Union gunboat *Essex* fired on Natchez, the only casualty was Rosalie, the seven-year-old daughter of Aaron and Fanny Beekman. Mrs. Nathan Lorie (née Miriam Wexler), a cousin of Rosalie who was nine years old at the time, wrote an account of how the family fled the Beekman home as the neighborhood was burning.

> We started to go down the hills, and I well remember how we rushed along, one behind the other. Rosalie was just behind me, and papa just ahead. I heard her fall and said: "Rosalie has fallen down." Papa called to her to get up. She said: "I can't, papa, I'm killed!" I remember [his] picking her up, his dreadful cries as he carried her in his arms, the blood streaming from her wound.

Rosalie, struck by a piece of shrapnel, died twenty-four hours later in the home of John Mayer.

Local historians report that Jews conducted orthodox services in Natchez as early as 1798, and had a cemetery on South Canal Street.

B'nai Israel of Natchez, established in 1840, is the oldest functioning Jewish congregation in Mississippi. In 1867 the congregation purchased a house and lot on Washington and Commerce streets for $2,500. Aaron Beekman, M. Lemle, David Moses, and Daniel Scharff signed a note for $1,300 at ten percent interest to facilitate the transaction.

Dr. Isaac Mayer Wise, rabbi and founder of American Reform Judaism, officiated at the cornerstone laying ceremonies for Temple B'nai Israel, which was built at the cost of $24,809.57. Dr. Max Lilienthal assisted the Reverend Aaron Norden, the new Natchez rabbi, in the temple dedication services in 1872. The following year, the congregation became a charter member of the Union of American Hebrew Congregations.

An often told story is that the choir, having no

B'nai Israel of Natchez, established in 1840, is the oldest functioning Jewish congregation in Mississippi.

music prepared for the first wedding ceremony at the temple, sang the hymn "Oh Lord, Be With Us Through the Long, Long Night."

The Reverend Dr. E. M. Rosenfelder served as spiritual leader of the congregation for several years and resigned in 1880 because of his defective eyesight (see Woodville).

The first temple building was destroyed by fire in 1903.

Next door to the temple stood this house, the "Parsonage." It served as the home of the early Natchez rabbis. In this city where fine, old homes are treasured, it is, at present, being renovated.

Plans for the rebuilding of Temple B'nai Israel were made two days after the first structure burned. Some non-Jews in Natchez sent donations to help their fellow citizens rebuild. The Methodist, Baptist, and Episcopal churches all offered their respective buildings to be used gratis. Selecting the first offer made, Congregation B'nai Israel met in the Jefferson Street Methodist Church until their new facilities were ready.

In 1905, a new temple was dedicated on the same lot at a cost of $27,110.

The altar shown here displays the various traditional ceremonial elements of the Jewish synagogue. Within the white marble ark one can find at least two Torahs, which contain the first five books of the Bible in Hebrew manuscript on parchment in the form of scrolls on wooden rollers. Above the opening to the ark, there hangs suspended the Perpetual Light. To the right of the ark, the initial words of the Ten Commandments are inscribed on a simulated form of the two tablets. To the left of the ark is the seven-branched candelabrum which signifies the six days of creation and the seventh day as the day of rest as indicated in the opening two chapters of the book of Genesis. This also holds for the candelabrum on a stand at the left. The candles on the low table to the left of the pulpit are the Sabbath candles. (The other lights are ornamental.) The high domed ceiling allows for the choir loft and an old pipe organ in the balcony over the altar, which is reached by a long flight of stairs.

Among the passengers on the sailing vessel that left Le Havre-de-Grace in 1833 on the uncomfortable, water-rationed, ninety-day trip to New Orleans was Jacob Mayer Levi (1806–1882). Some years earlier he had been discontented and had run away from his home in Landau to Paris. Because he was "afraid his father would find him and make him go home," the young man changed his name. The runaway son of Simon Levi and Janetta (Mayer) Levi and the grandson of Baruch Levi (1700–1756) and Fanny Levi (1704–   ?) dropped the family name when he stepped onto the boat and became John Mayer.

On the boat, John Mayer met fifteen-year-old French-born Jannette Reis (1818–1883) and her family. The young couple was married in 1835 in the Reis family home in New Orleans.

The John Mayer family moved in 1841 to Natchez where Mr. Mayer opened a fashionable shoe store. Their first home was on Main Street. During the Civil War, John Mayer invested his Confederate money in this house on Monroe Street.

Simon Mayer

The Mayer home, with its fourteen children and their friends, was filled with laughter, singing, and dancing, according to descendants. The door was open to all newcomers. The sons and daughters of John and Jannette Mayer married into other prominent Jewish families, and their combined influence on the Jewish community was remarkable.

John Mayer was the chairman of the first recorded congregational meeting held on September 8, 1861. This was not a new organization but an old group revitalized.

Major Simon Mayer, Confederate States Army, was born in New Orleans the son of John and Jannette Mayer.

Simon Mayer, a man of short stature (four feet, eight inches), enjoyed the army and advanced to the rank of major and aide-de-camp to General Sharp. Once, when the short, youthful-looking man was galloping on his big horse to deliver a message to his general's headquarters, a bullet passed through his high campaign hat, and observers reported his death. His mother and sister Emma were preparing to leave to claim his body when a telegram came with the happy news of his well-being. It seems his short stature and high hat saved the major's life.

Captain Steve Rumble and Captain T. Otis Baker, Natchez war comrades, often told stories of the "Little Mississippi Major" and of his kindness to the wounded. An often-repeated story was of his dismounting from his fine, big horse to let some wounded soldier ride while he walked alongside.

Simon Mayer and his wife Emma (Roos) had six children.

Natchez war comrades often told stories of the "Little Mississippi Major" and of his kindness to the wounded.

talented violinist who was also endowed with an excellent voice, he sang in the choir of a Cincinnati temple. Later the venturesome young man joined men headed west during the 1848 gold rush, but he found no gold and returned to the Midwest.

In St. Joseph, Missouri, he met Isaac Lowen-

Melanie Mayer Frank

Eleanor (Solomon) Reis (1777–1855), the wife of Moses Reis (1770–1835), was the mother of Jannette Reis who married John Mayer. Nobody in the city of New Orleans was orthodox enough to suit the bride's father, so Moses Reis performed the wedding ceremony for John and Jannette Mayer. At least seven generations of the Reis family have lived in the United States.

After the fall of Vicksburg, Union troops also took Natchez. It was then that three young men—Henry Frank, Isaac Lowenburg, and John Hill—came into the John Mayer store. They were sutlers, men who followed the troops and sold the soldiers small wares and provisions. Since armies had no commissaries for feeding their men, sutlers served an important role.

Henry Frank and Isaac Lowenburg introduced themselves as Jews and Mayer, who was the president of the Hebra Kadusha [Hebrew: Holy Society], invited them to join the local men at services held upstairs in the old engine house on North Union Street.

Henry Frank came to the United States from Hamburg, Germany, at the age of fourteen. A

burg, and the two men followed the army as sutlers until they settled in Natchez.

Henry Frank married Melanie Mayer, the daughter of John and Jannette Mayer. All the Frank children were educated in Boston. Their sons were sent to Phillips Exeter before going to college. Ophelia was sent to the Boston Conservatory of Music.

The Henry Frank Wholesale Dry Goods Building, 112, 114, and 116 North Pearl Street, had 25,000 square feet of floor space.

Courtesy *Natchez*, R. M. Hynes, photographer

Isaac Lowenburg (1836–1888) emigrated from Germany in 1858. He came with Henry Frank as a sutler with the Union Army into Natchez. Like his friend, he also married a daughter of the Mayer household, Ophelia Mayer, reportedly a high-spirited, ardent Southerner.

Ophelia and her friends had written a bundle of inflammatory letters about Generals Ransom and Brayman. The ladies were arrested and placed in confinement. After one day, Ophelia was released because of a high fever through the intervention of Lowenburg and Frank, who personally approached Lieutenant Parker, the officer of that day.

The Mayer house was sealed off by guards, and the business remained closed for three days. The store merchandise was not confiscated because of the intervention of their new Yankee friends.

Ophelia and Isaac were married in 1865 by their neighbor, Judge Thatcher, because there was no rabbi available. Several officers of the Federal Army who had befriended the family were invited to the wedding.

In 1870, the Lowenburgs went to visit his parents in Germany. They returned with a Torah, a gift of the Hechingen congregation to the Natchez synagogue. The Ullmans, Geisenbergers, and Benjamins, among others, had family connections in the same European community.

Ophelia Lowenburg (1845–1871) died at the age of twenty-six. Isaac Lowenburg later married Molcie Joseph. From 1882 to 1886 he served two terms as mayor of Natchez.

Wolfe Geisenberger (1819–1899) was born in Weisenberg, Alsace-Lorraine. This pioneer merchant was among the Jews who came to Natchez in the 1840s. His wife, Fannie (Netter) Geisenberger (1836–1904) was born in Schwindratzheim, Alsace-Lorraine. Fannie Netter's mother was Flora Ullman, who was a sister of Jacob Ullman, the patriarch of the Ullman family in Natchez.

Wolfe and Fannie Geisenberger came first to Port Gibson, where their oldest son, Ben, was born; they later moved to Natchez.

Sam Geisenberger, son of Wolfe and Fannie Geisenberger of Natchez, and Joseph Friedler, who married Ophelia Frank, daughter of Melanie and Henry Frank, were partners in Geisenberger and Friedler Cotton Factors and Wholesale Groceries.

Two unidentified students flank Dr. Isaac Mayer Wise, rabbi and founder-organizer of American Reform Judaism, and Rabbi Seymour G. Bottigheimer (1871–1930). Rabbi Bottigheimer was with Temple B'nai Israel from 1899 to 1913 during a period of great congregational growth. In those days when blacks suffered a demeaned status in the South, this rabbi invited Dr. George Washington Carver (1864?–1943), Negro agricultural chemist and educator, to occupy his pulpit. Despite the qualms of a few fearful souls, Dr. Carver was well received.

Ballroom of the Standard Club, which was on the second floor of the "Jan" Seiferth Dry Goods building

Rabbi Bottigheimer was with Temple B'nai Israel from 1899 to 1913 during a period of great congregational growth. In those days when blacks suffered a demeaned status in the South, this rabbi invited Dr. George Washington Carver, Negro agricultural chemist and educator, to occupy his pulpit. Despite the qualms of a few fearful souls, Dr. Carver was well received.

17

Phyllis Beekman was born in Natchez in 1897, the daughter of Dr. Phillip Beekman and Matilda (Haas) Beekman and the granddaughter of Aaron and Fanny Beekman. She married Daniel Scharff. The photograph was taken c. 1905.

Natchez was a village in 1843 when Aaron Beekman (1822–1901) came to the United States from Forets, Germany. His interest in the growth of the Jewish community prompted him to watch over the twenty-five children in the Hebrew School and to serve as secretary and president of the early congregation.

This store on Franklin Street, c. 1860, in the area known as Cotton Square, is where A. Beekman served as cotton supplier and broker.

His seven-year-old daughter, Rosalie, was the only casualty in Natchez during the war between the Union and the Confederacy.

Carl Lehmann (1847–1925), the son of Jonah and Julie Lehmann, was born in Landau, Bavaria.

His first stop was in Natchez in 1867; he married Clara Weiss, who was born in 1855 in Waterproof, Louisiana. The couple established Lehmann's Landing, where he operated a plantation. They returned to Natchez where he opened Lehmann's Jewelry Store. Carl Lehmann loved Natchez and was very active in the community.

Janet Mayar   Courtesy Naomi (Bock) Lehmann, Natchez

Janet Mayar, of Clinton, Louisiana, and the daughter of Henry L. Mayar, married Jonas Lehmann, the son of Carl and Clara Lehmann. In gratitude for her work in behalf of the Natchez congregation, a room in the temple was named in her honor and a memorial fund was established for the temple's upkeep.

Edward "Eddie" Schwartz and his children when they first came to this country from Europe. Mr. and Mrs. Schwartz had a women's apparel store on the corner of Union and South Franklin streets.

Photograph above and below courtesy of Mrs. Rae Frishman, Meridian

Granddaughter of Mr. and Mrs. Eddie Schwartz

Cassius L. "Cash" Tillman II, one of four generations born in Natchez, was the son of Cassius L. and Ricka Tillman.

The first Cassius was the brother of Joseph Tillman who arrived in Natchez c. 1843.

The Tillman family was related to the Isaac Rubels of Fayette and to Henry Marx of Port Gibson.

A scholar, author, and poet, whose words were printed in *Reader's Digest* and quoted by General Douglas MacArthur, Samuel Ullman (1840–1904) was an exceptionally talented man.

Ullman came from Germany in 1852 at age twelve with his parents, Jacob and Lena (Goldsmith) Ullman, to Port Gibson. The family moved to Natchez in 1865. He served in the 16th Mississippi Infantry Regiment, Confederate Army. After the war, he became president of the Jewish congregation at a time when it already had forty families. He married Emma Mayer, the daughter of John and Jannette Mayer.

In response to requests for aid from Confederate soldiers, Emma, her mother, and her sister contrived to take contraband through the Union lines. They asked Henry Frank to obtain a pass for them to visit friends. Under their wide hoop skirts, the Ullman ladies suspended shirts, boots, medicine, etc. When their carriage reached the city limits, Emma handed the guard their pass. According to Emma, the illiterate guard "tried to read the pass upside down." The trusting soul bade the ladies "have a nice day with your friends."

The Ullman and Laub sign reads "Plantation Supplies, Chewings, etc." Samuel Ullman and David Laub, the proprietors of the store at the northwest corner of Franklin and Commerce streets also sold dry goods and groceries. Their trade extended to planters of Jefferson, Franklin, Adams, and Wilkinson counties.

Courtesy Elaine (Ullman) Lehmann, Natchez

The first commercial venture of Marcus Maximillian Ullman and his cousin Isaac Laub began in 1875 in Madison Parish on a Louisiana plantation, in a store owned by the Britton and Koontz Bank.

According to the Natchez *Democrat*, M. M. Ullman and Company opened their store, shown above, in 1878 at the time when there were twelve other merchants on the same Commerce Street block in Natchez. With the exception of Ullman's, still operated by a member of the family, all the other original stores have closed.

Two father and son teams were the proprietors of M. M. Ullman and Company. From left to right at the top are Marcus Maximillian Ullman and his son, M. M. Ullman, Jr. At the bottom in the same order are Isaac Laub and his son, Alvin Laub.

Isaac Laub (1857–1931), the son of Sol Laub and Fannie (Ullman) Laub, moved from Goldman's Landing in Tensas Parish, Louisiana, to join his first cousin M. M. Ullman in business. Laub married Hattie Beekman (1862–1937), a native of Natchez.

Marcus Maximillian Ullman (1849–1926), was the son of Jacob Ullman (1805–1880) and Lena (Goldsmith) Ullman (1807–1873), and grandson of Ben Israel Ullman (1770–1820) of Hechingen, Germany. Marcus Ullman married Ella Victoria Sontheimer (1857–1920), a native of Lexington in 1881.

21

Ella Victoria Sontheimer

Marcus M. "Max" Ullman, pictured here as a boy, was the son of Ella Victoria (Sontheimer)

and her husband M. M. Ullman. "Max," their youngest son (1895–1945), was born in the family home on Monroe Street. He married Mildred Ehrman, the daughter of Henry and Sara (Gross) Ehrman (see Vicksburg and Canton).

The invitation to the golden wedding reception in the Shlenker home in Natchez—shared by the nine children, thirty grandchildren, and friends of Mr. and Mrs. Isaac Shlenker—had the unusual touch of "then and now" pictures.

The bride, Charlotte (Seeleman) Shlenker, who was the daughter of Baruch and Magdalena (Gukenheim) Seeleman, was born in 1838 in Kaiserslautern, Rheinpfalz, Germany. Isaac Shlenker, the groom, was the son of Cantor David Shlenker and Fanny (Elsaesser) Shlenker and was born in 1831 in Westhofen, Germany.

Isaac and Charlotte came with their young son to Harrisonburg, then Trinity, Louisiana. Isaac Shlenker was engaged in the mercantile and planting businesses and also served as postmaster. In 1888, the family moved and settled in Natchez where their children, David, Carrie (Hirsch), and Johanna (Geisenberger), were already living.

One of the grand old men of Natchez, David Moses (1821–1902), came to the village of Natchez from Sourbourg, Alsace-Lorraine. His wife, Babette (Gatzert) Moses (1824–1887), came from the same town.

D. Moses and Sons, "cheap cash store," general merchandise and cotton buyers, was a fixture in the rough-and-tumble section of Natchez-Under-the-Hill.

Both David and Babette Moses worked for the temple community. His interest was in the construction and maintenance of the temple, and her special interest was the Hebrew Ladies Aid Society. Babette (Gatzert) Moses, at left, and David Moses with his granddaughter Emma were true pillars of the Jewish congregation.

D. Moses and Sons, "cheap cash store," general merchandise and cotton buyers, was a fixture in the rough-and-tumble section of Natchez-Under-the-Hill.

Barnette and Emma, the children of Simon and Minnie (Loeb) Moses and grandchildren of David and Babette (Gatzert) Moses

Glen Auburn, the home of Simon and Minnie (Loeb) Moses, was built by the son of David and Babette Moses. The home is diagonally across from Temple B'nai Israel.

Minnie Loeb Moses, the mistress of Glen Auburn, admires her gown for the silver wedding anniversary of Simon and Minnie Moses.

The unusual dining room of their house featured a magnificent round table.

All through his years, S. L. Benjamin kept meticulous records of his favorite literature. The Spanish Hebrew poet Judah Halevi is mentioned frequently. Delicate paintings and drawings embellish many of his private papers.

At age seventeen, Samuel L. Benjamin (1838–1922), later known as "S. L.," left Alsace-Lorraine on a sailing vessel bound for New Orleans. The son of Abraham and Sara (Ullman) Benjamin was headed for Natchez, where his mother's brother Jacob Ullman and his family lived.

S. L. sent for and married his first cousin, Bettie Netter (1838–1925). She was the daughter of his mother's sister, Flora Ullman (1801–1871), who had married Baruch Netter of Alsace-Lorraine.

S. L.'s war service in the Confederate Army begun in 1862, ended with capture in Grand Gulf in 1863, and the young soldier was part of a prisoner exchange before the war was over.

The story repeated by a grandson to exemplify the spirit and mind of his grandfather recalls the time when S. L. and a local physician were walking together and talking in the area of the Moses home: "The two men wore flowing capes and tall hats. A Black man came toward them and stepped off the sidewalk into the gutter and tipped his hat saying, 'How do, Doctor; how do, Mr. Benjamin.' In response, Mr. Benjamin tipped his hat saying, 'How do, George.' The doctor turned to S. L. saying sharply, 'Mr. Benjamin, I do declare! I never did see a white man tip his hat to a neg-rah! Never saw such a thing in my life!' to which S. L. replied blandly, 'I just wanted to show I have just as good manners as he has.'"

All through his years, S. L. Benjamin kept meticulous records of his favorite literature. The Spanish Hebrew poet Judah Halevi (died c. 1140) is mentioned frequently. Delicate paintings and drawings embellish many of his private papers. Historians are grateful for his careful records of Jewish congregational meetings and precise recording of grave sites in the cemetery.

Interior of the "S. L." and Bettie (Netter) Benjamin home

Sara Abrams

In 1899, Helen Ione Benjamin, daughter of Bettie and Samuel L. Benjamin, married Moritz Louis Kleisdorf of New Orleans. The marriage ceremony was performed by Rabbi Bottigheimer. The bride, who was born in Natchez in 1877, attended Stanton College in that city. She lived to age ninety-two.

Jessie, Phillip, and Leon, left to right, were the Natchez-born sons of the Benjamins. Phillip (1864–1918) joined his father's wholesale liquor business when the firm moved from Main Street into the company's own building at 107 South Commerce Street.

Many of the peddlers who came home to Natchez after a week's work would gather at the Millstein house for the Sabbath.

On one occasion in the 1890s a special picnic was planned. The girls fixed lunch while some of the men went horseback riding. Sam Abrams was one of the riders. His horse moved so rapidly that he did not have the opportunity to duck under the overhanging limb of a large tree. As a result he was incapacitated for quite some time, and it was Sarah Millstein who took it upon herself to nurse Abrams back to health.

Descendants of their marriage—performed by Rabbi Seymour G. Bottigheimer—still live in Natchez. Sarah (Millstein) Abrams was the daughter of Feigha Millstein. Her husband, Mendell Millstein, was the son of Israel and Frieda Millstein of Rumania.

Helen Kleisdorf

Sam Abrams took over the Millstein store, which was on Franklin Street, when the Millsteins left Natchez.

Standing in front of the store is little Leon Abrams, holding onto his father's hand. As was common in that era, Sarah and Sam Abrams lived with their four sons upstairs over the family grocery and, as in many other small family businesses, the boys, as they grew older, waited on customers and made deliveries.

Their father died leaving many debts. The teenage Abram boys went to the creditors, Mr. Veiner and Mr. Seiferth of the Jewish community, and begged for the opportunity to run the store and pay off the business debts. The boys and their mother worked very hard and were not only able to pay off their debts but also to establish good credit and see their business expand.

Photograph of Abrams store courtesy Lawrence Abrams, Bay St. Louis, Mississippi

David Laub contentedly puffs his pipe while he poses with his grandchildren on the steps of his house.

Simon Moses sits on the steps of Glen Auburn holding his granddaughter, Jane Lois (Wechsler–Stein).

Isaac Schlenker with his grandchildren, David and Leah (Hirsch)

Southwest Mississippi

FAYETTE

Halfway between Natchez and Port Gibson is the town of Fayette, the Jefferson County seat, where several important Jewish families lived, conducted successful businesses, and fought side by side with their neighbors in the Confederate cause.

Courtesy Dr. and Mrs. Harry Greenberg, New Orleans, Louisiana

Ferdinand Krauss

In an interesting fabric of interrelationships, the sons and daughters of Jewish families of Fayette and vicinity found their spouses in the neighboring towns of Port Gibson, Grand Gulf, Lorman, and Natchez.

One such town was Union Church, near Fayette, where, according to genealogist Dr. Malcolm H. Stern, New York City, Daniel Hofheimer, an itinerant peddler, settled. His marriage to Rachel Marx in Vicksburg produced four children, all born in Union Church. Rachel died in 1861 and was brought to Natchez for burial in the Jewish cemetery. The defeat of the Confederacy sent Daniel back to Virginia where he and his four brothers later founded Hofheimers, the shoe store chain well-known in the Norfolk area.

Ferdinand Krauss, born in 1833 in Leimersheim, Rhein Pfalz, Germany, came to the United States in 1852, where he married Bertha Simon and moved to Fayette. He served in the "Chas. Clark's Rifles, of the Twelfth Mississippi Regiment in the Virginia campaign and was wounded in the Battle of Seven Pines."

S. Hirsch, born in 1848 in Alsace, Germany, came to the United States in 1872. Hirsch, a Fayette merchant, was a member of the board of aldermen and a trustee of the high school. He was vice president of the Jefferson County Bank, which, in 1904, proclaimed a capital of $25,000 and surplus and profits amounting to $10,000.

Shown here is S. Hirsch's store in Fayette.

This primitive photograph shows Estelle (Klotz) Mayer Levy, who was born in Alsace in 1821, and her daughter Julia. Estelle's first husband, Meyer Mayer, died in Grand Gulf from yellow fever six months after their daughter Julia was born in 1853. Estelle later married Mayer Levy. She owned much property both in Fayette and in Port Gibson where she died in 1892. Her daughter Julia married Henry Marx of Port Gibson and died there in 1913.

Estelle's great-grandson tells of a legal suit pressed by her second husband, titled *Mayer Levy* vs. *United States of America*.

"During the Civil War, General Grant sent General McPherson to the store for merchandise. He took a little less than $5,000 [in merchandise] including 100 pairs of ladies' shoes . . . valued at $1.00 a pair. [Neither] the USA nor the Union Army ever paid for the merchandise and, in the 1870s, Mayer Levy sued the USA in Washington. The original [document] is in the American Jewish Archives in Cincinnati. The plaintiff lost the case, because it was claimed that 'he was not a citizen at the time of the loss of merchandise.' How could he have been a citizen [of the United States] since Mississippi had seceded from the Union? The family claimed that they voted for Lincoln, supported the Union, freed their slaves before the war, etc. One former slave of my great grandmother so testified."

He also records: "Alcorn is a black college and the story told me was that my great grandmother, Estelle (Klotz) Mayer Levy, had educated a young slave as a musician, that she freed him (as they did the others prior to the war) so that he could teach music at Alcorn."

Isaac Scharff, shown around 1882 at age twelve, was the son of Daniel and Caroline (Wertheimer) Scharff of Fayette and Natchez. Isaac married Lena Laub of Natchez.

Caroline (Wertheimer) Scharff, born in 1830, was the second wife of Daniel Scharff. Daniel's first wife was a sister of Julius Weis. Daniel was a peddler and then a merchant who lived at times in Fayette and in Natchez. He is mentioned frequently in the 1866–1867 minutes of the Natchez temple.

Meyer Eiseman, born in 1828 in Meillinger, Bavaria, entered the United States through the port of New Orleans in 1846. He went first to Natchez in 1854, where he met and married Henrietta Weiss, the daughter of Abraham and Helena Weiss of Natchez.

Like many other immigrants to the South, Meyer Eiseman began as a peddler. When he had saved $1,500, he went into business in Fayette with Julius Weis, an equally remarkable man, in 1853. Their individual business ventures constitute real "American success" stories. Julius Weis sold out to Meyer Eiseman during the yellow fever epidemic in 1875. Eiseman eventually became the head of an extensive mercantile firm.

At his death in 1881, the *Fayette Chronicle* wrote about him: "Of a quiet and unofficious dis-

position, a liberal mind and a kindly heart, he won, in his early days in this county, the respect and esteem of all classes of our people, who feel no shame in mourning his loss as a sincere friend and one of the best citizens."

Judge Jeff Truly of Natchez reminisces in a letter written to Clara Eiseman Scharff, Eiseman's daughter, on the occasion of her eightieth birthday. He writes about the "great good which the Jewish merchants did to the town of Natchez, Fayette, Rodney, Union Church, and Port Gibson, before, after, and during the Confederate War and throughout the . . . days of . . . Reconstruction . . . Your father confined his works to Fayette and Jefferson County."

The Judge continues: "He was a member of the Democratic Executive Committee for the entire Congressional District, and his voice was as the voice of thousands. . . . Another characteristic of your father was his attempted concealment of his own generous remembrances. . . ."

Peddling in the day of Julius Weis was made difficult when the Mississippi legislature raised the license fee from $20 to $100 per year. Weis eventually came to Fayette and opened a store in partnership with Meyer Eiseman in 1853 and went to Natchez to buy stock from the firm of Meyer, Deutsch & Company. Deutsch invited Weis to come into the business in Natchez, and Weis later sold out to Eiseman. Before he accepted the offer, however, he had earned enough money so that he could return to Germany to visit his parents. When he returned to Natchez, Weis learned that Deutsch had moved to New York city, and Weis took over the entire business.

In his memoir, written 1908–1909, Weis recalls, as a young peddler, his horrified reaction to the punishment of a slave who was "whipped upon his bare back by an overseer." Later, when a customer named Jeffries followed the trail of twelve runaway slaves with bloodhounds, he recalls that one of the Negro women "came up to me and asked me to protect her from the dogs. I told her that I would if I could, but before we got to the house the dogs overtook her, and before the men arrived they [the dogs] had torn almost every thread of her clothing and bitten her se-

Julius Weis

verely. Altogether this was a very disagreeable and repulsive scene to me."

In 1864 he married Caroline, the daughter of John Mayer, one of the early Jewish settlers of Natchez. They moved at a later time to New Orleans, where he became a very successful cotton broker and one of the city's renowned philanthropists.

Bertha (Wertheimer) Rubel was born in Fayette in 1841. At the age of sixteen she married Gabriel Meyer of Pine Bluff, Arkansas. She said many years afterwards that more than half of the people at the wedding in Fayette were dead two months later from yellow fever.

The Meyers' son, Isaac Rubel Meyer, moved to Port Gibson and married Hortense Marx, a native of that town. Descendants of their union still live in this part of the state.

Isaac Rubel, the father of Bertha, was an important citizen of Fayette. He was born in Kaiserslautern, Bavaria, in 1820. He married Amelia Wertheimer, who was born in Stollhofen, Bavaria, in 1824. They lived first in Rodney, then in Fayette, where he was in business with Joseph Tillman, a cousin from Natchez.

LORMAN

The town of Lorman was established in 1884 when a railroad company bought the property from the Hayes family. L. Cohn and his older brothers, Herman and Joseph, had started the Cohn Brothers store in 1875. L. Cohn eventually became sole owner of the store. The *Fayette Chronicle* states, "It can be truthfully said Mr. Cohn made Lorman what it is." Below are the Ellis Hotel and the store owned and operated by L. Cohn.

Isaac Rubel

"The Old Country Store . . . on US 61, is one of the Nation's oldest general merchandise stores in continuous operation. Among the fixtures in use since the store was built in 1890 are a shoe case with a windup motor to revolve the display, thread cabinets and two jewelry cases. The antique cheese cutter is still used to sell hoop cheese. There is a museum with mementoes of the past. Mon.–Sat. 8:30–6, Sun. and holidays noon–5; closed Easter and Dec. 25."

Tour Book, American Automobile Association

Courtesy *Architecture in Claiborne County*

RODNEY

A few Jews had lived in Rodney since 1820. Others merely made the town on the banks of the Mississippi River a stopover while they searched for livelihoods.

Jeremiah Chamberlain organized a church and then a school of higher learning in Rodney. The school attracted boys and girls who could not go to the schools in the East. By 1860, Rodney had a railroad, two warehouses, and a boat landing, with a population of 4,000.

Isaac Rubel worked in the flourishing river town before going to Lafayette. The Haas family had a general store in Rodney, but in 1870 the river began to change its course and moved inland. Little is known of the Haas family background, except that Minna (Levy) Haas was originally from New Orleans. In the 1880s the Haas store was covered, like others, by the river waters. Mr. and Mrs. Haas and their two daughters moved to Natchez and opened their new business near A. Beekman's on Franklin Street. One of the Haas daughters married a member of the Beer family. The other daughter, Matilda, married Dr. Phillip Beekman, son of Aaron Beekman.

PORT GIBSON

The curve of Bayou Pierre in the Mississippi River was where Samuel Gibson came in 1788 to claim his Spanish Land Grant. The town built on that land, Port Gibson, spared by General Grant on his march to Vicksburg, was declared by him "too beautiful to burn."

The busy riverport city attracted Jewish merchants in the early 1830s. Some of them came to Port Gibson from Grand Gulf, six miles away, which also had an early Jewish population. Grand Gulf even had its own early Jewish burial grounds.

The formation of Gemiluth Chassed Congregation took place in 1859 when twenty-two charter members met to conduct services in the Odd Fellows Hall until they could build a house of worship of their own.

"The view is from the roof of the Claiborne County Courthouse looking south along Market Street, c. 1906. The Fair Street intersection is near the center of the photograph" (Ed Polk Douglas, *Architecture in Claiborne County, Mississippi*, 149). The Harris Frishman store can be seen on the northeast corner of the intersection in the downtown area of Port Gibson.

Courtesy Herbert M. Meyer, Detroit, Michigan

The Meyer-Marx Drug Store, which stands at 625–27 Market Street, is "the only ante-bellum structure surviving in downtown Port Gibson."

According to *Architecture in Claiborne County*, "its architectural details indicate a construction date of 1830, making it another survivor of the great fire of 1939. The delicate keystones above the windows and the fan lighted triple windows are particularly fine."

Samuel Bernheimer (1812–1888), born in Hohenems, Tyrol, Austria, and his wife, Henrietta (Cahn) Bernheimer (1827–1904), born in Wittgenborn Kuhrhessen, Germany, came to Port Gibson in the 1840s. Their home at 216 Walnut Street, which was, according to descendant Carl Weil, used by General Ulysses S. Grant as his Port Gibson headquarters, burned down in 1900.

Just down the street in the business district, Samuel Bernheimer erected this building in 1876. At various times it housed the Bernheimer mercantile firm and the Cotton Exchange. *Architecture in Claiborne County* describes it as follows: "This building is an interesting example of the High Victorian Italianate style popular in the United States between 1860 and 1880. The style is characterized by the use of segmental or straight-sided arches and elaborate classically inspired detail. Both are seen here. The window lintels, store front, and roof cornice are prefabricated cast iron. The elaborate interior fittings remain, even though the structure is no longer in use."

Jacob Bernheimer (1863–1911), the son of Samuel and Henrietta Bernheimer, was born in Port Gibson and was, like his father, an excellent businessman. He was a benefactor of the Chamberlain-Hunt Academy (Presbyterian), a Mississippi preparatory school located in his home town.

The Bernheimers were leaders within the Jewish community and outstanding in civic life.

There were Jewish merchants in Port Gibson in the 1830s, but it was 1859 before Gemiluth Chassed Congregation was formed by twenty-two charter family members and began to conduct services in the Odd Fellows Hall. An obviously later list with no date shows a membership of forty-one family members.

N. A. Son, president of the congregation, awarded a contract to J. F. Barnes Company of Greenville, Mississippi, to erect a Jewish house of worship at the south end of Church Street. The architecturally unique Victorian Moro-Byzantine Revival temple, built 1891–1892, is topped by a steeple and dome of Moorish design. Imported crystal chandeliers adorned the sanctuary. The ceremonies were planned by N. A. Son, presi-

Courtesy *Architecture in Claiborne County*

dent; B. H. Levy, vice president; and the building committee, consisting of Emanuel Keifer, Jacob Bernheimer, William Cahn, L. T. Newman, L. M. Heidenreich, and H. Marx.

At the dedication, an antique crown, a breast plate, and a pointer for the Torah were given to

Congregation Gemiluth Chassed by Isidore Newman of New Orleans in memory of her parents, Mr. and Mrs. Louis Keifer.

The congregation joined the Union of American Hebrew Congregations [Reform] in 1874. The congregation's first spiritual leader was a rabbi from Austria. Rabbi Max Raisin, depicted in the Meridian section, also served this congregation.

Prior to 1830 burials were made in the Natchez Jewish cemetery, but in 1870 the Port Gibson Jews dedicated a local site for their use. Old records and bank books reveal that members of the cemetery association paid $2.50 per year for the upkeep of the grounds. Out-of-town members paid somewhat more. With the dwindling of the Jewish community in later years, the cemetery funds were left in trust with the Southern Mississippi Bank of Port Gibson in order to provide for continual future care.

E. Crysler, editor of the *Port Gibson Reveille*, stated in an interview: "Before 1910, the general population began to decline. By World War I, Claiborne County lost forty percent of its population, because of migration from rural areas and with it most of Port Gibson's Jewish population."

Temple Gemiluth Chassed stands today a vacant and unused building amid ante-bellum homes, as a tourist attraction—a lonely vestige of a proud people.

Henry Marx (1853–1904) came from Ingenheim, Rhein Pfalz, Germany, in 1869 to Port Gibson. He owned a livery stable as well as mercantile interests.

In 1872 he married Julia Mayer. After she had grown old, she told her grandson that his grandfather, Henry Marx, used to walk the distance (about seven miles) between Grand Gulf and Port Gibson, there and back, every day to see her before they were married.

Henry Marx, a prominent businessman who served as a town alderman, a trustee of the town schools, and as county supervisor, gave much time and effort to civic activity in Port Gibson, his home for thirty-five years.

Jacob Metzger Marx (1808–1899) and Anna (Weis) Marx (1811–1894)

Their three sons, Henry, Sol, and Theodore, lived most of their lives in Port Gibson. Henry, the youngest son, followed his brothers, who preceded him there by twenty years.

Hortense Marx of Port Gibson married Isaac Rubel Meyer (1870–1960), who was born in Pine Bluff, Arkansas. He was the son of Gabriel and Bertha (Rubel) Meyer. Bertha was born in 1841 in Fayette, Mississippi, the daughter of Isaac Rubel and Amelia (Wertheimer) Rubel.

Isaac Rubel Meyer, a pharmacist and a member of the Marx family, owned the Meyer-Marx drug store.

Courtesy Herbert Marx Meyer, Detroit, Michigan

Photographs courtesy Herbert Marx Meyer, Detroit, Michigan

Hortense Marx

39

Abraham Titche

Hortense Marx (1880–1945) and her sister, Rose (1884–1974), the daughters of Henry and Julia Marx

Hortense married Isaac Rubel Meyer; Rose married Jacob Bernhold. Like most of the members of the Meyer, Marx, and Rubel families, they are interred with their loved ones in the Port Gibson Jewish cemetery, which is at 900 Marginal Street.

Abraham Titche (1846–1928) was born in Venningen, Germany. He married Ida Levy (1861–1929) who was originally from St. Louis. The Titche family traces its history back to Reb Gershon Ashkenasy (1590–1660) of Debrzyn (Russia-Poland area). The name Titche first appears in the family genealogy with Abraham Titche (1628–1703). Titche evolved from the word *Deutsch*, the German word for *German*. Mississippi offspring of Abraham and Ida Titche still live in Natchez, Lorman, Vicksburg, and Clarksdale. The Titche Department Store in Dallas, Texas, was founded by descendants of the Titche family of Port Gibson. This house was built c. 1890 by Abraham and Ida Titche.

Ida Titche

Their son, Henry Titche Levy, shown here as a boy, was born in 1887 in Port Gibson. At his death in 1954 he was buried in the Port Gibson Jewish cemetery in the Titche-Levy family plot.

Jeanette (Titche) Levy (1863–1888) was born in Waynesboro and died in Port Gibson four years after her marriage in 1884 to Ben Levy.

The plaque in front of the Levy home, which is part of the Port Gibson Historic Tour, states: "LEVY HOME, 1202 Church. Ca. 1890. Stick Style. This house with its tall proportions, irregular silhouette, projecting eaves, and exposed framing in the gables is an interesting example of the Stick Style."

Shown here is Rosa (Miller) Bock, the wife of Felix Bock. She was not Jewish, yet a daughter spoke of the many times her mother went with her to Temple and of Rosa's commitment to rear the children as Jews.

Albert Bock, pictured here, and his wife Francis came from Germany to New York City where they lived and died. Their son, David, left New York to move to Port Gibson where he opened a general merchandise store next to the Meyer-Marx drug store. Felix, a half-brother to David, also left New York, but he settled elsewhere.

The Bock store in Port Gibson prospered, and Felix joined David in partnership.

David Bock's wife Esther died and, grief-stricken, he sought a change of location, moving to Vicksburg where he eventually remarried.

Photographs courtesy Naomi (Bock) Lehmann, Natchez

Intermarriage was a rarity in those days. The young people of German Jewish families of Mississippi, on the whole, managed for several generations to find mates among their own.

Vicksburg

In 1790 the Spaniards obtained a land grant from the Indians and built a militarily advantageous fort on the high bluffs overlooking the Mississippi River. The spot was named Walnut Hills by men on the flatboats that plied the river, because of the numerous walnut trees. The expanding city was later named Vicksburg to honor the Reverend Mr. Newitt Vick, a Methodist minister who, in 1814, established one of its first missions.

Walnut Hills was the early business district where the German Jewish merchants had their stores long before the city was incorporated in 1825. According to Vicksburg historian Gertrude Philippsborn, there were by then approximately twenty Jewish families in Walnut Hills, which became the modern business section of the city.

With the advent of the river steamboat on the Mississippi, settlers poured in from the eastern seaboard. The men of the "flat-bottoms" transported merchandise from Europe through the Port of New Orleans.

In addition to the boisterous flatboat group, there were wealthy planters and Choctaw Indians who came to town to make their purchases.

Immigrants, including Jews, made up another component of the Vicksburg community. They came from Poland and Germany to escape the poverty, the restrictions, and the harsh conscription laws of their homelands.

When the War Between the States began, young Jews responded as gallantly as did their neighbors to the call for enlistment in 1861. The first soldier to be wounded in the Battle of Vicksburg was Philip Sartorius, a local merchant. Louis Hornthal, one of the early Jewish arrivals in Vicksburg, was the last of the city's Confederate veteran soldiers to die.

Despite the pangs of growth, the Jewish population in Vicksburg grew, and by 1866 there were ninety Jewish families and approximately thirty-five Jewish-owned stores.

Between the years of 1820 and 1840, the Jews of Vicksburg gathered for worship in various homes. When their numbers increased, Bernard Yoste, who arrived in 1830, offered the upstairs hall of one of his buildings on Levee Street to his fellow worshippers.

When the time came for them to direct their attention to the building of a house of worship, wrote Gertrude Philippsborn in *The History of the Jewish Community of Vicksburg*, "The necessary funds [$25,000] for the building of the Temple had to be raised, and immediately thirty-nine pews were sold for a total of twelve thousand dollars [$12,000] while the other necessary thirteen thousand dollars [$13,000] were raised through voluntary contributions by the members of the congregation. In 1868 land was deeded to Levi N. Lowenberg, president; Samuel Fischel, secretary; Jacob Blum, Morris Mendelsohn, and Jacob Strauss as trustees of the congregation."

Photograph courtesy Harold Gotthelf, Jr., Jackson

In 1870, members of the congregation and their invited guests assembled on Washington Street to form a processional to go to the dedication service conducted by the Reverend Dr. Lilienthal of Cincinnati, Ohio, and by Dr. Bernard H. Gotthelf, the incumbent rabbi.

According to Mrs. Philippsborn, the *Vicksburg Herald* reported that the Order of Procession was as follows: "Police . . . Music (Jaeger's Brass Band of New Orleans) . . . Youth of the Congregation . . . Invited guests—Clergy in carriages—invited City and State officials in carriages (which included Governor and Mrs. Alcorn; General Carlin, the commander of the local Post; Honorable Charles Foster and other members of the Legislature; the Mayor of Vicksburg and the Councilmen; the Honorable H. R. Pease, State Superintendent of the Public Schools; members of the school board; of the Masonic and Odd Fellow lodges; and of the clergy of all denominations with the exception of the Catholic Priest, rode in 24 carriages which brought the invited guests to the Temple . . . Scroll bearers . . . Boys carrying tapers . . . Girls carrying wreath of flowers . . . Girl carrying the key on a cushion, encircled by four girls with a wreath, supported by two boys, carrying the national flag . . . Officers of the Congregation . . . Building Committee . . . Ar-

riving at the Temple the head of the Procession opens file, while the rear walks through and enters the Temple."

The altar and ark of the building completed in 1870 are shown above.

The land on which the Jewish cemetery of Vicksburg is located was part of the battleground during the siege of Vicksburg in 1863. The blood of men in both blue and the grey uniforms was shed on this tract of land.

Men from Alabama, Mississippi, and Texas clashed with five regiments of Union soldiers from Illinois and regiments from other states. The fierce battles devastated the land owned by Harris and Henrietta Kiersky and Elias and Caroline Kiersky, two Jewish families in Vicksburg.

In 1864, the Kiersky families agreed to sell this land, marred by gun emplacements and trenches as well as tunnels dug by Union troops,

The Jewish cemetery, adjacent to the Vicksburg National Military Park, has placed amid Jewish family graves several large memorials that recount the military maneuvers at each location.

to the Anshe Chesed congregation, to be used by its members as a cemetery, for $1,000.

The cemetery, adjacent to the Vicksburg National Military Park, has placed amid Jewish family graves several large memorials that recount the military maneuvers at each location.

Rabbi Bernard H. Gotthelf (1819–1878) was born in Bavaria and came at the age of twenty-one with his wife Sophia to the United States in 1841. Sophia Landau (1821–1917) married Rabbi Gotthelf at Binswanger, Germany, in 1839.

Keneseth Israel Congregation, of Philadelphia, Pennsylvania, was his first charge before he was called in 1851 to serve Adath Israel Congregation in Louisville, Kentucky.

At the request of the Louisville Jewish Community, Gotthelf was appointed by President Abraham Lincoln to serve as a United States Army chaplain. This appointment of the second Jewish chaplain in the history of the United States helped establish the right of rabbis to serve as military chaplains alongside their Christian counterparts. *The Louisville Journal* reported: "*An Excellent Appointment.*—We are

gratified to announce that President Lincoln has appointed the Rev. B. Gotthelf, the minister of the German Jewish Congregation of this city, as Hospital Chaplain, to be stationed here. The fact that a very respectable number of Jewish soldiers have been and still are receiving medical treatment at our hospitals having been brought to the notice of the Hon. Robert Mallory, he made an application for the appointment of Mr. Gotthelf, which we took pleasure, with other citizens, in endorsing . . . and we are, therefore convinced that the appointment was as timely as it is well merited." (Cited in *American Jewish Archives* I., 1.)

After the war, the Reverend Gotthelf came with his wife and their eight children to assume charge of Anshe Chesed Congregation of Vicksburg for the sum of $40 per month. He served his

---

At the request of the Louisville Jewish Community, Gotthelf was appointed by President Abraham Lincoln to serve as a United States Army chaplain. This appointment of the second Jewish chaplain in the history of the United States helped establish the right of rabbis to serve as military chaplains alongside their Christian counterparts.

---

community in Vicksburg until 1878, when he was a victim of the yellow fever scourge. His tombstone epitaph epitomizes him: "a wise teacher, a faithful minister, a devoted father, a good man."

Emma Gotthelf, the daughter of Rabbi and Mrs. Gotthelf, married Joseph Hirsh, a prominent Vicksburg lawyer, who was the son of the Hirsh family who originally came to Sallis (Mississippi) in the early 1840s. Hirsh was a member of the board of directors of the temple in its early history.

This house, known as "The Castle"—which has since burned—was the home of Joe and Emma (Gotthelf) Hirsh. Sophia Gotthelf, the

wife of the rabbi, lived the last ten years of her life with the Hirsh family. Because of the rabbi's chaplaincy, his widow received $20 per month as her pension from the United States government until her death in 1917.

"Uncle Hirsh" of Sallis, the father of Joseph Hirsh, brought three young members of the Forscheimer family to the United States. The first one, Carolyn, married Samson Weiner (see Canton). Nannie Forscheimer never married and lived with the Weiner family in Canton all her life. The third member of the family brought here

by "Uncle Hirsh" was Ben Forscheimer, who settled in Summit. Mrs. John C. Covington, in her talk to the Summit Civic Garden Club in 1945, referred to Ben, among others, who "rendered valiant service to the cause of the Confederacy."

Harold Gotthelf, born in 1891 in Vicksburg, was the son of Isaac and Bertha (Epstein) Gotthelf. Young Harold's picture was taken in 1894 when he was age three. He was the grandson of Rabbi and Mrs. Bernard H. Gotthelf of Vicksburg.

Edward Klaus (1856–1926) came from Germany in 1872 at the age of sixteen and became a United States citizen in 1884. He came to the Kraus family [note difference in spelling] in Fayette. His mother's maiden name was Kraus. Klaus stayed with the Kraus family for a while in order to learn English.

This photograph, showing Edward Klaus standing in the back row center, was taken in Vicksburg in 1880 shortly before his marriage to "Lena" Magdalena Shlenker in Natchez. He died

while at work on his plantation in Cary and was brought back to his home in Vicksburg where he was interred.

"Lena" Magdalena (Shlenker) Klaus (1867–1899), the daughter of Isaac and Charlotte (Seeleman) Shlenker, was born in Trinity, Louisiana, and later moved to Natchez with her family. In 1886 she married Edward Klaus, Sr., in Natchez. They lived in Vicksburg where Lena died at a very early age.

Known as the "B B Club," the B'nai B'rith Literary Association of Vicksburg was formed in 1896 "for the purpose of the intellectual and social advancement of its members."

Known as the "B B Club," the B'nai B'rith Literary Association of Vicksburg was formed in 1896 "for the purpose of the intellectual and social advancement of its members." Its membership was "confined entirely to Israelites," according to its constitution. The club's first property, purchased for $10,500, was a lot facing on Cherry and Crawford streets. The original building was destroyed by fire and a new, handsome marble structure was built on Clay and Walnut streets. It had an indoor swimming pool on the lowest level. The main floor had meeting rooms, a library, and a fine dining room. A ballroom with a gilded ceiling and elaborate chandeliers was on the top floor.

The opening ball at the second "B B Club" building, pictured here, was a gala attended by many Jews from the surrounding area.

The members of the confirmation class of 1907, with their beloved Rabbi Sol Kory, bear the family names of many original Vicksburg Jewish families: Jack Schwartz, Minnie Rose, Amelia Levy, Henry Foster, Matille Klaus, Carrie Orbach, Mathilda Beer Hirsch, Inez Levy, and Adele Klaus, who married Harold Gotthelf, Sr.

Rabbi Solomon Lysander Kory (1879–1936) was born in Coffeeville, Mississippi. He was the son of Abraham and Caroline (Lichtenstadter) Kory. Abraham Kory was born in Prussia in 1837 and died in Vicksburg in 1924.

Rabbi Kory was a graduate of the University of Cincinnati, and he attended graduate school at the University of Chicago. He was ordained in 1903 by the Hebrew Union College of Cincinnati, Ohio. In 1904 he married Katherine Braham, who was born in 1879 in Cincinnati. (*History of Mississippi*, Dunbar Rowland.)

In addition to tending to the spiritual needs of members of Congregation Anshe Chesed, he went once a month to both Greenwood and Lexington to conduct services in these small communities.

When this much-admired rabbi died, the *Vicksburg Evening Post* reported on his funeral in these words: "The sun shone brightly, and all about were the beauties of nature, as the last rites and vows were spoken and the body of Rabbi Kory consigned to the grave. All this seemed symbolic of Rabbi Kory's life and character, who had served Anshe Chesed Temple for over thirty-three years."

Leon Fischel and his brother Sam are mentioned in the memoir of Phillip Sartorius. The brothers, who came from Alsace-Lorraine, served in Company A, the Fifteenth Louisiana Battalion, Cavalry. Leon Fischel, pictured in his uniform, was an aide to Albert Sidney Johnston, Confederate States Army.

The little boy depicted here with his arm resting on the table was named Albert Sidney John-

ston Fischel, a namesake to honor his father's commanding officer.

A. S. J. Fischel, the son of Leon Fischel, married Stella Abrams of Port Gibson. The Abrams family is to be found on the original membership list of the Port Gibson congregation. Fischel operated the Pearl Laundry on Mulberry Street in Vicksburg.

Lee Kuhn

Lee Kuhn was born in Vicksburg the son of Alexander and Caroline Kuhn. Alexander Kuhn (1835–1888) was born in Essingen, Germany, and his wife Caroline (1839–1919) was born in Klingen on the Rhine. They came to Vicksburg in the 1860s where they had a dry goods store. Their three sons remained bachelors, but their two daughters married.

When Lee Kuhn died, he left the bulk of his estate, $400,000, to the City Catholic Charity Hospital with the proviso that other money from government sources would be obtained and added to it to build a new hospital building to honor the members of his family. He stated specifically that the hospital was for the underprivileged "of all races, creed, and color."

Kuhn bequeathed to the temple the sum of $20,000 with the provision that the income be used for underprivileged children in the vicinity.

When Lee Kuhn died (a bachelor), he left the bulk of his estate, $400,000, to the City Catholic Charity Hospital with the proviso that other money would be obtained and added to it to build a new hospital building.

The temple fund is still intact and a committee oversees the distribution of warm clothing and special needs upon request from needy families.

Mose Hornthal, a member of the family of Louis Hornthal. The latter was a well-known Vicksburg Confederate soldier who fought in the Virginia campaign. He was one of the original founders of the "B B Club" in 1871.

Courtesy Jack Rice, Vicksburg

One of the early Vicksburg furniture stores of the company founded by David Rice in 1868

David Jacob Shlenker (1865–1913), cotton merchant. His large warehouse was near the river bank overlooking the Mississippi River.

Alice (Kiersky) Meyer (1850–1938), a native of Vicksburg, was the daughter of Harris and Henrietta (Rothschild) Kiersky.

The two Kiersky brothers, Harris and Elias, are on record among the founders of Temple Anshe Chesed. In 1864 they sold to the congregation the land that was to be used as a cemetery.

Mrs. Meyer's father, Harris Kiersky, became a naturalized citizen in 1856, and his brother, Elias, followed suit three years later in 1859.

Alice (Kiersky) Meyer, who was said to have been an outstanding pianist, was raised in a house near the river banks that stood as a bulwark against the advancing army in 1863.

These photographs show two finely preserved large lithographs of David Rice and of his wife, Pauline (Cromline) Rice, of Vicksburg. The portraits are part of the collection of the Mississippi State Historical Museum in Jackson.

The genealogy of the three historic Judah, Gomez, and de Lucena families traces the family of Pauline Cromline back to its arrival in this country in 1665 at New Amsterdam (New York City).

The tragedy of the war between the North and the South can be seen in the Cromline family history: two sons served in the Union Army while their daughter, Pauline Rice, resided in the staunchly Confederate city of Vicksburg.

David Rice (1842–1889), the son of Isaac Rice, left Ingenheim, Germany, with his two sisters about 1860. He worked in Louisiana before he came to Jackson and then came to Vicksburg in 1865. By 1868, David Rice had accumulated enough capital to open the first post-war furniture store in Vicksburg.

Pauline (Cromline) Rice (1847–1926) was born in New York City. She was the daughter of Amelia Emily Judah (1806–1877) and Rowland Cromline (1804–1872), both of whom were native New Yorkers.

When one traces these families it becomes clear from the names and places of origin that this was a family of Marranos (Jews who, during the Spanish Inquisition, sought to avoid death at the stake through becoming converts. *Marrano*, literally, is the Spanish for "pig.") The family

must have either left Spain or was expelled during the Inquisition of the fifteenth through the seventeenth centuries.

Their wanderings across Europe, as evidenced by their countries of birth, match the pattern described by historians. The last piece of the puzzle fits when one notes that the son of Moses de Lucena, namely, Abraham de Lucena (1635–1676), was born in Brazil, arriving in New Amsterdam in 1655. According to Jewish historians, the first Jews to come to North America came during that era in 1654 from Recife, Brazil.

Noteworthy on the genealogy is the name of Baruch Judah, born 1679 in Breslau, Germany, who was made a freeman in New York in 1716. It can be surmised that he came here as an indentured servant, as was the common practice in those days, and worked a number of years to pay for his passage.

His son, Samuel Judah, who was born in 1728 in New York and died in 1781 in Philadelphia (Pennsylvania), is noted on the genealogy as a "patriot and signer of [the] Nonimportation Agreement protesting British Tax; helped finance Revolutionary war."

A strange odyssey for the antecedents of two families: Spain—Italy—Holland—Germany—France—London—British West Indies—New York—Philadelphia—Vicksburg, Mississippi!

Sol Fried came from Bavaria about 1870 at the age of eleven. He married Rose Beer, who was born in Magnolia, Mississippi, the daughter of David and Melanie (Kahn) Beer who originated in Bavaria.

Sol and Rose (Beer) Fried and their family, shown here, came to Vicksburg in 1895.

Marks Sokolsky and three sons

Rose and Phillip Sartorius

Marks Sokolosky (1832–1889), the son of Israel Sokolosky, was born in Prussia. He married Henrietta Levy, the daughter of Micah Levy, in 1857 in New Orleans.

The Sokolosky family came to Vicksburg about 1870, where they established the M. Sokolosky dry goods store. One of the three sons in the family was confirmed by Anshe Chesed Congregation. Sokolosky was a member of B'nai B'rith Lodge #98 in Vicksburg.

In 1910, Phillip Sartorius (1831–1913) wrote his memoir, from which the following information was gathered (courtesy, Dan Scharff, Jr., New Orleans. Also published in *Memoirs*.) The original manuscript was written with his left hand because his right arm was injured during the Civil War. Sartorius means "tailor" in Spanish. The Sartorius family had migrated during the time of the Inquisition from Spain to Germany.

Phillip Sartorius was born in Germersheim on the Rhine, Bavaria, Germany. His brothers, Isaac and Jacob, already settled in the New

World, encouraged him, although he was only fourteen years old, to join them. His parents were loath to let their "youngest and only son at home" leave but they consented. So in 1845 he and an older sister, Caroline, left their homeland to go to Vicksburg, Mississippi, where Jacob had migrated two years before. They also had a sister, Mrs. Kohlman, in Benton, Mississippi.

The brother and sister embarked on the sailing vessel called *Taglioni*, bound for New Orleans. They sailed from Europe in mid-September and arrived at their destination the first of November. From there they took the packet *Concordia* to Vicksburg.

Jacob Sartorius had previously brought a Torah with him to Vicksburg. Phillip, too, brought a Torah from Germersheim. Both Torahs are still in the possession of the Vicksburg congregation.

In 1854, Phillip married Sophie Rose (1835–1910), who was born in Spiza on the Rhine, Germany, and they were married for fifty-six years. In the course of twenty-five years they had nineteen children, six of whom died early.

His service in the Confederate Army was painful, both physically and spiritually. He despised the carnage, the waste of men and material, and the injustice of man against man. He writes frankly of the utter disregard that Confederate soldiers had for their fellow Southern soldiers and citizens. He learned that his wife and children were innocent victims of the callousness inflicted upon them by soldiers on both sides of the conflict. When Yankee soldiers looted stores, "what they could not or did not care to take away, they threw on the floor and poured tinctures over them."

According to his memoir, Phillip Sartorius was the first man shot in the battle at Millikin's Bend near Vicksburg. The bullet which lodged at the end of his shoulder blade was removed by "a young excuse of a surgeon of an Indiana regiment . . . He had no instruments with him but an old rusty pocket knife."

The Valley Dry Goods Company on Washington and South streets was founded by Simon Switzer in 1881. He came from Staunton, Virginia, to Vicksburg and married Flora Leyens of that city.

Edgar Leyens, the brother of Flora (Leyens) Switzer, joined the company almost at its inception; the third generation of this family is still involved in this highly successful business venture known locally as "The Valley." This is the original Valley Dry Goods Company.

The Switzer-Leyens family portrait. Front row, left to right: Edgar Leyens, Babette (Bloom) Leyens, and Walter Leyens. Back row, left to right: Eugene Leyens, Flora (Leyens) Switzer, and Harry Leyens.

Babette (Bloom) Leyens (seated in the wicker chair), born in Bavaria in 1829, was the matriarch of the Leyens-Switzer family. She was the wife of Louis Leyens, who enlisted in Grenada in the 28th regiment of the Mississippi Cavalry A in 1862. He served the duration of the war while his wife and their children went to live at Grand Isle near Port Gibson where they lived until hostilities had terminated. Mrs. Leyens died in Vicksburg in 1908.

Mr. and Mrs. Martin Baer of Rodalben, Germany.

Below is the house of their son, Francis, at 1104 South Street in Vicksburg. Francis Baer

(1826–1885) married Theresa Meyer (1830–1896), who was born in Aubersweiler, Germany. They were the parents of Carrie (Baer) Leyens.

Carrie Baer married Edgar Leyens, a leader in business and civic activities, in 1898. Their two sons, Francis (sitting in the cart) and Louis (standing near the toy horse) joined their father in "The Valley," the family business.

Francis attended Phillips Exeter and graduated from Yale. His brother Louis was a graduate of Cornell University.

Maurice Brown Emmich (1900–1963) was the descendant of two pioneer Jewish merchant families in Vicksburg. The picture shows his grandmother, Rosa Brown (1845–1926), sitting on a carnival crescent moon holding another grandchild, Rose (Emmich) Foote.

His paternal grandparents, the earliest members of the Emmich family in Vicksburg, were Morris Emmich (1826–1876), a master builder (cabinet maker) from Germany, and his German-born wife, Sara (Simmons) Emmich (1838–1898). They had five children—one son, Sam Emmich, who was born in Vicksburg in 1869, married.

Sam Brown, Sr., (1845–1922) married Rosa. Their daughter, Helen, born in 1875 in Vicksburg, married Sam Emmich, the son of Mr. and Mrs. Morris Emmich.

Maurice B. Emmich owned and operated the Emmich Insurance Company. He was a member of the Mississippi Bridge Commission when the bridge was a toll bridge. In addition, Emmich was the chairman of the Kuhn Memorial Hospital Committee. This group raised sufficient funds, after the bequest of Lee Kuhn, to build a million-dollar hospital to replace the oldest section of the

Photographs courtesy Ann (Grundfest) Emmich, Vicksburg

Maurice Brown Emmich

Rosa Brown with her grandchild

institution. Fannie, the sister of his grandmother, Rosa, married a member of the Kuhn family.

Robert Emmich, the son of Mr. and Mrs. Maurice Emmich and a great-grandson of the Emmich-Brown families, married a Grundfest from Cary. He was president of the temple. There are great-great-grandchildren of the original Brown and Emmich families living in Vicksburg today.

One of the most colorful families in Vicksburg history, the Ehrmans, is featured in an article called "Vicksburesque," written by "V.B.R." for the local newspaper. The clipping is not dated.

"The Ehrmans were among the most remarkable men in Vicksburg's commercial history. When their advertisement way back in 1895 designated them the 'Largest Meat Dealers in the South' it probably was right."

Jake, Albert, and Henry, the proprietors of the chain of nine meat markets, were the sons of Charles and Clara (Ehlbert) Ehrman, who came to the United States from Alsace-Lorraine. Charles Ehrman served as a member of the state legislature in Jackson.

"Vicksburesque" continues: "In the long stretch of years over a half-century ago when whole venisons, whole bears and wild fowls of all sorts hung up in the front of Vicksburg meat markets, the name of Ehrmans was famous for hundreds of miles up and down the rivers . . . the Ehrmans gave more meat away free than many of us had in a month. . . ."

The Ehrman markets filled their retail, wholesale, and steamship company orders in a manner no longer possible in today's business. Cattle from beef-raising states escorted by "herders and drovers" rumbled down the streets of Vicksburg to the accompaniment of shouts and whistles. "In those days, with little or no game restrictions . . . professional hunters . . . brought in wild geese, ducks, quails and sometimes bears and deer . . . with innumerable rabbits. . . ."

Jake Ehrman, the youngest of the three brothers, a bachelor, eventually moved from Vicksburg to Jackson where he opened a meat market (see Jackson). Albert Ehrman, who married Esther Lasker of Little Rock, Arkansas, was the most sports-minded of the three excellent businessmen. He sponsored and outfitted a baseball team and kept a fine stable of horses.

Henry Moses Ehrman, the oldest son of Charles and Clara Ehrman, was born in Ocean Springs, Mississippi. Prior to his marriage, he served the Confederacy under the command of Albert Sidney Johnston. He married Sara Gross (1864–1944) the oldest daughter of another Con-federate veteran, Charles L. Gross, and his wife, Sophie, of Canton (see Canton).

This young girl with the flowered parasol over her bicycle is Mildred (Ehrman) Ullman Kern, the daughter of Mr. and Mrs. Henry Ehrman. She married Maximilian Ullman, Jr., of Natchez in 1917 (see Natchez).

Photographs courtesy Elaine (Ullman) Lehmann, Natchez

56

The Delta

YAZOO CITY

This city, which stands on the banks of the Yazoo River was first occupied by white men in 1824. Two yellow fever epidemics, in 1853 and 1878, struck the town, wiping out entire families in some instances.

Shortly after the Yazoo River overflowed its banks in 1882 and destroyed a large portion of the city, Jewish merchants came in during the rebuilding period. They stayed on to help rebuild

after a fire destroyed all of the business district and a large part of the residential section.

When he was five years old, William Hirsch (1878–1945) was brought to New York City from Germany by his maternal grandmother, Minna Littman. He was the son of Meyer Hirsch (1850–1922) and Rose (Littman) Hirsch (1845–1904) of Berlin.

At the turn of the century, William Hirsch and his wife, Ella (Littman) Hirsch (1880–1906), came to Yazoo City. (The two Littman families were not related.) Because the city was, for a

William Hirsch

Ella Hirsch

Courtesy Joan (Ascher) Cahn, Meridian

time, a railroad center, his general merchandise store, like many others, depended on the trade of railroad employees and their families.

Yazoo City had many Jews who passed through the area over the years. Solomon Davidow lived there for a while in the 1880s with an uncle and his brother Marcus before going to Belzoni. Among the people who stayed a short time and those who were permanent residents, there was a sufficient number to gather for the Holy Days in private homes for services.

Jewish businessmen like William Hirsch and Sol Summerfield were active in the business community and in the Masonic order.

CARY

The main occupation in the town of Cary and its environs was the growing of cotton. Before the Yazoo and Mississippi Valley Railroad was built in 1883, cotton was hauled by wagon to the river front to be shipped down the Mississippi River. If the roads were passable, sometimes the farmers stored their cotton and hauled it to Deer Creek, where it could also be shipped by steamboat.

Among those who came to farm cotton was one of the sons of Isaac and Charlotte Shlenker of Natchez.

One of Cary's largest growers was an early Jewish settler, Morris Grundfest, who was born in Russia in 1869. He met his Russian-born wife in a rather strange manner. In the 1880s in New York City, a friend asked him to do a favor: to go to the incoming boat to meet a young lady named Molly Bernstein. He did, and she soon became his wife.

Morris and Molly Grundfest came to Mississippi, where he was a peddler. In 1895, they settled in Cary, where they placed their general store in the railroad zone.

Sam Fielding Lamensdorf, born 1898, was the son of Ben and Lizzie (Borodofsky) Lamensdorf.

The Lamensdorf, Borodofsky, and Grundfest families still have strong family and business ties in the Cary and Rolling Fork area. The original parcel of land purchased by the Grundfests con-

Sam Fielding Lamensdorf

tinues to be farmed by their granddaughter, who married a member of the Lamensdorf family.

ANGUILLA

Even before it was called Anguilla, a Jew named Ben Pearl had come, in 1875, to this snake-infested canebrake territory. Mail came by horseback every six weeks, and the settlers were cut off from the outside world. In 1888, when the railroad came through, the name Anguilla was given to the town. The railroad brought a few other Jews. Because there were too few to establish a Jewish house of worship, Henry and Dora Kline would gather all the Jewish children in the vicinity into their home where he taught them Sunday School lessons.

Henry Kline was born in 1870 to a farming family in Lithuania. An older cousin, Ben Pearl, sent for the young man to join him in cotton farming in Anguilla. Together they established a store now known as Kline's department store. Henry sent for his brother Meyer and helped him

Photographs courtesy Frieda (Kline) Fischel, Vicksburg

Dora Adelson Kline and daughter, Frieda, Anguila

settle first in Mayersville and then in Alligator, Mississippi.

In 1903, Henry Kline married Dora Adelson in St. Louis.

He was a member of the P.M.A. Board [Pure Milk Association] and the chairman of the Sharkey County Democratic Party.

The family moved to Vicksburg in 1921 to provide a better secular and religious education for their children. He drove over gravel roads one hundred miles daily, round trip, to oversee his farmland and business in the lower Delta.

An active participant in Vicksburg Jewish functions, he served on the board of the Anshe Chesed Congregation and was an honorary president of the Jewish Welfare Board.

Upon his death in 1953, the Grundfest family of Cary named the temple they had built in Rolling Fork the Henry Kline Memorial Congregation in tribute to the man who had befriended them years ago when they first came to this area.

NITTA YUMA

White men first came to this heavily forested Indian territory in 1768, according to James F. Brieger, in his volume *Hometown Mississippi*. Even when Charles Blum came in the mid 1880s to Nitta Yuma, it was still a sparsely populated, virgin Mississippi Delta region. He came first to Vicksburg in 1873 and he peddled a wide area, moving his family about in the state for several years until he finally opened a store in Nitta Yuma.

Charles Blum photograph courtesy T. K. Griffis, Masonic grand secretary, Meridian

Photographs courtesy Mrs. A. W. Freyman, Greenville

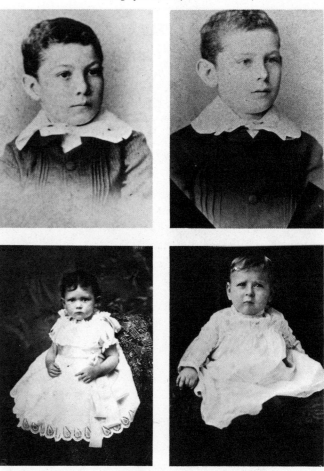

Top, left to right: Moise, born in Lauderdale in 1878; Marks, born in Rolling Fork, 1880. Bottom, left to right, Sara, born in Anguilla in 1883; Jacques, born in Nitta Yuma in 1886.

Charles Blum's six brothers cast their lot with France during the Franco-Prussian War. He was too young to enlist with them but, during the siege of Paris, he was permitted to leave the city to sell French pastries to the German officers. Because he knew German, he could pass on valuable information to the French. Charles Blum (1856–1924) left France abruptly in 1873 one step ahead of the Germans, who would have shot him as a spy.

At a later time, when Mr. and Mrs. Blum were quite well settled in Nitta Yuma, they went on a trip to Strasbourg, where he was promptly arrested by German authorities. Because he was already an American citizen, this almost caused an international incident.

During his peddling days, Charles Blum met and married Rebecca Yaretzky, the daughter of Marx Yaretzky (see Shuqualak).

It is possible to follow the Charles Blum family's quest for a livelihood by noting the places where their four children were born along the way.

CHATHAM

Chatham was a small village twenty-six miles south of Greenville and near Lake Washington where keelboats used to haul freight. The cotton plantations and settlers in the area frequently depended on peddlers to obtain supplies.

Mr. Stein came into the Chatham area as a peddler. He opened this store, which was later photographed by Dan Guravich and put on a calendar. The Stein family also farmed cotton nearby on 345 acres. The family is related by marriage to the Cohn-Davidow family in Belzoni (see Belzoni).

Courtesy David Davidow, Greenville

that is still called "Sontheimer's Place," even though the family no longer owns it.

Congregation Beth El [Hebrew: House of the Lord], consisting of about thirty Jews, built its temple in 1904 on a lot on Spring Street donated by Morris Lewis and Sam Herrman.

Lena Levy, a native of Vicksburg, organized a local amateur group to put on a show for the benefit of the Temple. The show, the talk of the town for many years, yielded $164.

The Temple's fiftieth anniversary was attended by people from every denomination of Lexington as a tribute to this small group of solid, contributing citizens.

This small congregation continues to have a rabbi come in monthly.

Abraham Herrman (1833–1924) was born in Hainoxhorah, Bavaria. He married Celia Sontheimer (1847–1912), a native of Lexington. The Herrmans moved from Davisborough, Georgia, to Lexington, where some of their descendants still live.

LEXINGTON

The trading post of Lexington was given the status of city in 1836. At about the same time, Jacob Sontheimer, who was born in Germany in 1819, came to Lexington and opened the first brick store on the town square. Jacob and his wife, Mary, purchased their first land in the early 1840s; they built a 1200-acre cotton plantation

Courtesy Fay (Lewis) Berman, Lexington

Morris Lewis, Sr., and Sam Herrman

Sam Herrman (1877–1936) was born in Davisborough, Georgia. This photograph was taken when he married Flora Levy of Vicksburg in 1898. He is buried in the Jewish cemetery of Lexington.

At age thirteen, Morris Lewis (1873–1959) left Poland and came to New York. Four years later, with almost no formal education, he went to Sidon, Mississippi, to clerk in a relative's store for $25 per month. It was in Sidon that he met Julia Herrman, a granddaughter of Lexington pioneer Jacob Sontheimer.

M. Lewis, shown at left, had saved $500 by 1896 and moved to Lexington to go into business with Sam Herrman, shown at right, Julia's brother. Lexington had no synagogue at the time, so Morris Lewis and Julia used the facilities of the newly built Methodist Church for their marriage in 1900.

The little grocery business evolved into the Lewis Grocer Company. With Morris Lewis as president, the Sunflower Food Store chain was established. Sixteen years after the death of Lewis, the company did $180 million worth of business a year.

It was Morris Lewis, Sr., who helped Lexington get its first cotton compress, first cotton oil mill, first ice factory, first waterworks and sewage system, and first electric light plant. The hospital, the schools—every civic endeavor interested the busy man.

It was Morris Lewis, Sr., who helped Lexington get its first cotton compress, first cotton oil mill, first ice factory, first waterworks and sewage system, and first electric light plant. The hospital, the schools—every civic endeavor interested the busy man.

62

In 1905 he helped organize the Merchants & Farmers Trust Company of Holmes County and served as its president. During the depression of the thirties, he mortgaged everything including his home and put up his stock in the Lewis Grocer Company as a guarantee. He told his children, "I am doing this to protect depositors in the bank and make good on my commitments to our farmer customers. It was they who had suffered losses during the previous year because of the severe drop in the price of cotton. If things do not work out for the best, I may not have much in material wealth to leave you when I die; but I promise I will leave you the greatest wealth one can own—and that is a good name."

Isaac Flower and his wife Esther came from Poland to the United States in 1881 and eventually settled in Lexington, Mississippi.

Isaac Flower started a store involved in the sale of "misfit clothing." He was a vest cutter in Poland and "could take a size 40 suit and cut it to size 36."

The Flower store, as you can see, did not sell flowers. The family name in Poland was Kwiat, from the Polish word for *flower*.

Both Isaac and Esther were among the organizers of the congregation and founders of the temple.

H. A. Rosenthal, a member of the firm of Rosenthal Brothers

Rose and Bettie, the daughters of Jacob (1819–1886) and Mary (1821–1891) Sontheimer, at the turn of the century had a successful business called R & B Sontheimer Company, "Furnishings." Bettie (Sontheimer) Fisher, pictured here, was the general manager.

In that cotton growing area, "furnishings" indicated a distinct service, namely, the furnishing of supplies of all kinds to tenant farmers, or sharecroppers. The latter would turn over half of the crop to the landowner in return for the use of his land. The furnishing of farm and family needs could also be charged against the tenant's crop. This included meat to be salted down, coffee, sugar, bolts of cloth, infant items, seed, and mules. For the inevitable, the tenant could buy coffins. At harvest time, repayment came out of the tenant's half.

Brought to this country by an aunt, Isadore Hyman came in the late 1850s to Greenwood, Mississippi. He later married a descendant of Jacob and Mary Sontheimer and joined the R & B Sontheimer Company, "Furnishings." He became an owner of much farmland, farming 4,000 acres using tenant farmers or sharecroppers.

When a girl who worked on his land bore an illegitimate child and did not want the baby, he assumed its care. He had in effect a small, private orphanage where a woman took care of these unwanted children. He provided food, shelter, and clothing for them until they were able to go out on their own.

Courtesy Herbert A. Hyman, Lexington

BELZONI

In the middle of the nineteenth century, Belzoni had no doctors, schools, or churches. After the Civil War, two Jewish families named Livingston and Morris came to operate stores and grow cotton. By the late 1880s, other Jewish families came into the now enterprising community, and soon there were enough men to form a *minyan* (a religious quorum of ten men) for worship in private homes.

In the small Mississippi River town, business houses were located facing the river. The town sprang to life when the calliope of the showboat could occasionally be heard, for it promised days of shows and special treats for the townspeople.

Morris Cohn and his sons had one of the oldest dry goods and grocery establishments in Belzoni. His wife was a daughter of the Stein family of Chatham. His daughter Frieda married Solomon Davidow, who had an adjoining mercantile store.

Photograph courtesy *The Greenville Times*

GREENVILLE

Solomon Davidow and his bride Frieda Cohn of Belzoni. Solomon Davidow was born in Russia-Poland in 1859 and arrived in the United States in 1880. He went to an uncle in Pulaski, Tennessee, and then to Yazoo City where his brother Marcus and another uncle lived. Belzoni became the Davidow home in 1892.

The Davidow Dry Goods store founded in 1892

Courtesy Mamie Davidow, Laguna Hills, California

Blantonia, the plantation established by Colonel William W. Blanton in 1828, was the place where Morris Weiss opened his store in 1864. By 1865, the Mississippi River town of Greenville was formed on Blantonia and was dedicated by Harriet Blanton Theobald, the Colonel's widow.

As Greenville grew, these names appear among its most active and influential citizenry: Marx Gunsberger, L. Witkowski, M. Morris, Julius Landau, Theodore Pohl, Leon Moyse, Nathan Goldstein, and Jacob Alexander. The latter served as mayor of his city and concerning him, Herman W. Solomon wrote: "In 1876 the *Times* recorded one of the last hurdles of carpetbaggery [that] Greenville had jumped, the confirmation of Jacob Alexander as Postmaster, 'an event which gave satisfaction to the community after a carpetbagger who served. . . .'"

Jewish community life began with Congregation B'nai Israel, which was loosely organized in 1869.

There were major calamities that affected the citizens of Greenville: the Civil War, the Great Fire of 1874, and the yellow fever epidemic of 1878.

During the war in 1863, Greenville was destroyed; undaunted, the people wasted no time and rebuilt the town. Despite warnings of community leaders against fire hazards, people built houses and places of business out of wood. The Great Fire consumed forty-five dwellings and sixty-two business establishments. Twenty-five business places were owned by Jews, most of whom had minimal or no insurance.

The year 1878 was to be remembered as the year when the yellow fever struck the alarmed population. In desperation people tried every rumored and recommended potion and preventative. Frantic doctors, ignorant of the cause, advised, among other things, reduced bathing, the drinking of brandy, and the avoidance of all alcohol. Patients were advised to use mustard plasters and, despite the August heat in the Delta, the wearing of woolen stockings.

Yellow fever killed thirty-three percent of the town's approximately 2,000 people. The Jews of

Greenville counted eighteen of their number among the casualties.

Once again, Mrs. Theobald provided land from Blantonia, this time to establish a burial place for the unfortunate. The citizens divided the land into three segments. One third was devoted to burial of the blacks and another third to the whites. The middle section was assigned to the Jews. There were just a few Chinese, which seemed to present a problem. They were buried in the Jewish segment.

The Greenville Times reported: "Mr. John Manifold [a non-Jew], our undertaker, who has been worked hard ever since the epidemic, finished his labors on earth last night and will receive his reward in heaven."

Organized Jewish religious life in Greenville began when a group of orthodox Jews established Congregation B'nai Israel from 1869 to 1879 and had Rabbi Charles Rawitzer of Memphis, Tennessee, serve on a part-time basis as their religious leader.

In 1879, as more Jews came into Greenville, the congregation reorganized under the name of Hebrew Union Congregation. The newly organized group built a building of wooden construction about 1880 on the corner of Main and Hinds

Courtesy Rosalie Moyse Raphael, Greenville

streets on land donated by a non-Jew, Harriet Blanton Theobald, known, because of her generosity, as the "Mother of Greenville." This building was evidently designed primarily as a school, because private schools were then the chosen means for instruction, with a small portion of the building set aside for religious purposes.

Courtesy Hebrew Union Congregation, Greenville

On the same site, a new house of worship for the Hebrew Union Congregation was built in 1906. The new temple, complete with sanctuary, religious school facilities, and a meeting hall, cost $30,000. The handsome brick and stone structure based on Grecian architectural design was patterned after the temple in Natchez. Rabbi Joseph Bogen was the first permanent rabbi of the Greenville congregation. Significantly, the congregation began using for its prayerbook the new *Minhag America*, the American rite. Greenville's congregation counts among its members Jewish families from surrounding small towns over a wide area.

Morris Weiss came to this country from Neustadt, Prussia, and landed in New York City. He made his way to New Orleans and then peddled his way into the Mississippi Delta. He set up his first store in 1864 on the Blanton plantation. Weiss, the first Jewish merchant in Greenville, married Hannah Neuman. Young Nathan Goldstein joined the Weiss dry goods enterprise in 1868. The Weiss and Goldstein families played an important role in the growth of Greenville.

After her husband, Morris, died, Hannah Weiss, shown in this 1863 photograph, joined her son-in-law Nathan Goldstein in managing their business. She was a highly capable, self-confident person who admired these same qualities in her son-in-law. They were a high-powered team, whether engaged in business, a community endeavor, or the raising of funds for the temple.

Hannah Weiss had a mind of her own. All her life she adored Queen Victoria and, since her brothers in Germany had a lace factory, she had them copy the Queen's lace pattern for her own use. In addition, dinner plates for the family china were copies of the British Queen's pattern.

Hannah Weiss had a mind of her own. All her life she adored Queen Victoria and, since her brothers in Germany had a lace factory, she had them copy the Queen's lace pattern for her own use. In addition, dinner plates for the family china were copies of the British Queen's pattern.

This strong-willed, intelligent eccentric who reigned as the matriarch of her large family subscribed to the *New York Times*, which came to Greenville by river boat. A descendant reports: "No one in the family dared touch her paper until she had read it through thoroughly."

The interior of the Hannah Weiss home in 1895 is shown ready for a reception honoring the engagement of her granddaughter, Edna Goldstein, to Rabbi Abraham Brill, the spiritual leader of the Hebrew Union Congregation.

The Weiss home as it was on Washington and Theobald streets

Members of the family are seen gathered around "Grandma" Hannah Weiss at her home in 1895. The children and grandchildren assembled are members of the Witkowsky, Witt, Goldstein, Brill, Hirsch, and Moyse families who married into her family.

Most of these family members lived in Morris and Hannah's home even after they married. The cousins were very close and got along very well. A granddaughter commented years later, "They wouldn't dare be otherwise."

Nathan Goldstein

Courtesy Rosalie (Moyse) Raphael, Greenville

When the South was still in the throes of reconstruction after the war, Nathan Goldstein maintained his composure and was helpful where he could be. When it became obvious that a judge was obviously corrupt, Goldstein was a member of the committee to set things right. When the town of Greenville was in confusion because of the yellow fever in 1878, the city government operated with a skeleton group of officials led by Goldstein.

At the turn of the century, Greenville built a new high school complete with a modern gymnasium at the corner of Starling and Main streets, and Nathan Goldstein gave his city $10,000 to equip it. A plaque was affixed to the gymnasium wall to honor the benefactor for his gift.

The Greenville Times, in 1907, reported: "It cannot be denied as a fact that it has been to the liberality of Messrs. Blum and Goldstein that many of the wealthiest and most successful planters in this and Bolivar county today owe much of their success and prosperity."

His generosity and willingness to lend money to the needy without collateral affected his finances. Many people were unable to repay their debts to him so that, although he certainly did not die a poor man, he lost much of his land and other property.

The Greenville Times, *in 1907, reported: "It cannot be denied as a fact that it has been to the liberality of Messrs. Blum and Goldstein that many of the wealthiest and most successful planters in this and Bolivar county today owe much of their success and prosperity."*

Lula Witt, front center, in a prenuptial picture at the time of her marriage in 1890 to Julius Phillips. The only bridesmaids that can be identified are standing in the back row. Beginning at left, they are Edna Goldstein Brill, Camille Goldstein Moyse, Sadie Witt, and Rachel Alexander Weiss.

Jane (Riteman) Goldstein Woolf (1831–1910) was born in Russia-Poland. Nathan and Sara Goldstein were the children of her first marriage.

When her husband died and she could not provide for the children, they were placed in an orphanage in New Orleans. While living at the orphanage, Nathan, a precocious youngster, set up at age fourteen a stand in the French Quarter of New Orleans to supplement family needs.

Mrs. Weiss, the matron at the orphanage, had a son, Morris Weiss, who had a store in Greenville. Nathan, now a charismatic young man of eighteen, went there in 1868, applied for and obtained a job. He also won the boss's daughter; in 1876, he married Emaline Weiss.

Jane Goldstein Woolf

Five members of the 1890 first graduation class of Greenville High School were Jews. The girls, back row, left to right, are Belle Marshall, Amelia Morris, and Ella Sievers. In the bottom row left is Lula Witt and at the right is Moses Landau. The Jewish community gave up their sponsorship of the private school, in line with the tradition of learning as found in the book of Deuteronomy: "Thou shalt teach . . . thy children."

In 1907 the *Greenville Times* wrote about Sol Brill as follows: ". . . coming to this city in the year 1874 from Union Town, Ala., where he clerked in one of the large stores of that city, he opened up a store of not little size on Mulberry street, which street is now in the river. Fifteen years later he moved . . . and in 1890 he again moved to his present large quarters. In all these years, through yellow fever, high water, overflows, and money panics, Mr. Brill has remained a true and loyal citizen to Greenville."

69

The Leyser store was one of three large department stores in Greenville before the turn of the century. It was founded by David Leyser. At the time of the 1907 souvenir edition of the *Times*, L. Riteman, who was a director on the board of the Citizens Bank, was in charge of the store.

Leon Fletcher was part owner and manager of the Greenville Steam Laundry. The previous laundry building owned by Fletcher and Harris was destroyed by fire. This picture displays the new laundry built in 1907, which boasted "five washing machines; two centrifugal extractors; and a steam drying room which dries in thirty-five minutes."

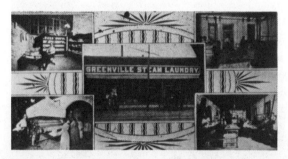

Leon Fletcher was born in 1867 and died in Greenville in 1933.

The Nelms and Blum "Fashionable Emporium of Greenville" was one of two nineteenth-century stores there that continued into the twentieth. Sam Blum was the Jewish partner who, when Nelms retired, became president of the firm. The store was located on the corner of Washington Avenue and Shelby Street. In 1907 it was pro-

claimed as "the only store in Greenville handling exclusively ladies' and children's goods, and making a specialty of these lines, enables them to show a most attractive stock." The store was later purchased by Charles Hafter.

Charles Hafter was born in Alabama. He went to Meridian in 1878 and, in 1886, he left for Greenville. Hafter acquired the Nelms and Blum store. Its outgrowth, Charles Hafter's Emporium of Fashion, continued in the city at 10 Walnut Street.

Photographs courtesy *The Greenville Times*

In its day, the Roslyn Hotel had the reputation of being the finest hotel between Memphis and New Orleans. It was said that its dining room "was the delight of gourmets far and wide."

Morris Rosenstock was a prominent planter in the county before he moved to Greenville in 1905. He was one-third owner of O. B. Critten-den and Company, cotton factors and commission merchants.

The Hotel Cowan became the Roslyn Hotel when it was purchased by Leon Fletcher: "Ros-lyn" was the acronym for Rosa, his wife, and Leon, his son. In its day, the Roslyn Hotel had the reputation of being the finest hotel between Memphis and New Orleans. It was said that its dining room "was the delight of gourmets far and wide."

Courtesy *The Greenville Times*

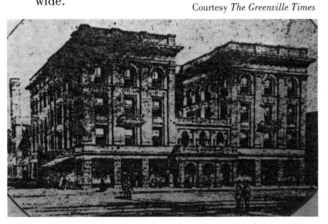

H. Wilczinski was president of District #1 of the board of supervisors of Washington County and also served as a member of the city council. When the Jewish congregation received its char-ter in 1880, he was its treasurer.

Herbert H. Hirsch sold fresh native and Kan-sas meats in his market, which was considered the most up-to-date in the state. His son was Dr. Jerome Hirsch. Herman W. Solomon wryly com-mented that the doctor "got good practice in dis-section in the family meat market and became the first Jewish physician in the city."

B. B. Goldman was born in Louisiana and came to Greenville when he was very young. Ac-cording to the *Greenville Times*, "In 1896 he suc-

B. B. Goldman

Goldman liquor store

Photographs courtesy *The Greenville Times*

ceeded the late Theo. Pohl [a pioneer Jewish citizen of Greenville] who had conducted a wholesale liquor house at 307 Washington Ave-nue for many years." He was a prominent mem-ber of the Cotton Pickers, the then famous Elks Lodge of Greenville, and served a term as its Ex-alted Ruler.

Hodding Carter tells how Joe Weinberg's faith in him saved his newspaper from falling into the hands of a not too scrupulous stockholder.

The Greenville Times tells about Maurice A. Bergman in these words: "[He] spent all of his life in Greenville, except during the Spanish-American War, while the Delta Guard were in camp. After being mustered out of service, he entered the employ of his captain, Capt. Henry T. Ireys, Jr. . . . [After the latter died] he purchased the business, which is the oldest insurance agency in the Delta and probably one of the oldest in the State."

The Joe Weinberg building was built by Joe, the son of Isaac and Yetta Weinberg. The Weinbergs arrived in Greenville about 1875.

Maurice A. Bergman

Courtesy *The Greenville Times*

Herman W. Solomon wrote, "Against the advice of friends, in 1911 he built the only 'skyscraper' since the erection of the Cowan Hotel . . . His philanthropies were many . . . Hodding Carter, in 'Where Main Street Meets the River' tells how Joe Weinberg's faith in him saved his newspaper from falling into the hands of a not too scrupulous stockholder."

The H. Scott family came to Greenville in 1867. They established two saloons. One was known as The Cotton Exchange and was on Washington Street. The other was called Scott's East End Saloon. Scott was the agent for the Pabst Milwaukee Brewing Company.

CLEVELAND

In its early days, logs were cut with hand saws until the railroads laid tracks to haul machine quarter-sawed oak logs out of Cleveland. From 1886 to 1900, the town was built around saw-mills. It was to this community, where men carried guns for protection, that Leon W. Kamien moved his family from Durant.

By 1921, enough Jews were there and in nearby towns to combine efforts, establish a congregation, and build a synagogue. Temple Adath Israel (Congregation of Israel) was built in 1927 and, a year later, the congregation engaged Rabbi Jacob Halevi as its first rabbi.

Tillie Kamien was born in 1894. She was the oldest daughter of Mr. and Mrs. Leon W. Kamien of Cleveland, Mississippi. Tillie married William B. Morrison, and they farmed land on the eastern side of Cleveland where they also owned a little grocery store.

Tillie Kamien Morrison

Photograph courtesy Rachel Miller Baskind, Greenville

Maude Hilda Kamien was born in 1898 in Boyle, Mississippi, the daughter of Mr. and Mrs. Leon W. Kamien. She is shown with her Cleveland high school graduating class and is seated at the right. Not long afterwards, Maude Kamien became Mrs. Abe Miller.

In 1892 the first Kamien store was opened. The second store, built in 1904, was the first brick building built in Cleveland, built at a time when the town's streets were dirt and the sidewalks were of wooden construction. There was little law enforcement, and Leon W. Kamien, a pioneer merchant, found it necessary to carry a gun for protection. There were no banks in Cleveland and, according to his son, I. A. Kamien, Sr., "when he went to St. Louis to market, he carried his money in his shoes."

Shown here is the interior of the 1904 store. From left to right are Thomas Wilson, I. A. Kamien, and Mr. and Mrs. Leon Wolfe Kamien.

Photograph courtesy Rachel Miller Baskind, Greenville

The surname of the family of Leon Wolf Kamien (born 1861) was evidently derived from Kamien, the town in Poland where they lived. Rachel Reichenberg, who later became his wife, was born in Germany in 1865. Leon and Rachel Kamien came at first to Durant, Mississippi, and then settled in 1892 in Cleveland, Mississippi, where they remained. There they began a store which has been operated by four generations of the family. The original Kamien family donated land for the building of the local Methodist and Baptist churches.

Sophie Reichenberg, who was born in 1875 in Germany, married Emil Sealbinder, and they operated a dairy farm near Cleveland where her sister, Rachel Reichenberg Kamien, lived. The Sealbinders lived in Durant before coming to Cleveland.

Photographs courtesy Rachel Miller Baskind, Greenville

BEULAH

Many steamers docked at the boat landings of the cotton plantations surrounding the town of Beulah where Samuel Meyer Baskind had his store. In coming to this country, Baskind had "jumped the ditch" in order to avoid being conscripted by the Russian army. He came first to Alligator, Mississippi, and then, after his first wife died in childbirth, he moved to Beulah.

Florence Wachenheim, poet, was born in 1885 in Vicksburg and was the second wife of Samuel Meyer Baskind.

GRENADA

Initially, two rival speculating companies formed two separate towns that became, in the 1830s, the one town of Grenada. Dispute continued, however, between the two groups until the Civil War compelled a union of the quarrelling forces.

In the 1850s, the names of Wile and Ginsburger appear in the *Grenada Sentinel*, the town newspaper. Max Ginsburger was lauded as a very active citizen; Meyer Wile was an active Mason.

The devastating yellow fever epidemic in 1867 struck almost half of its 2,500 citizens, with 326 deaths.

Isabella Streng Wile, the daughter of Fannie and Joseph Streng, was born in New York City in 1838. After her marriage to Meyer Wile of Grenada, Joseph Streng came in the 1850s to be near his daughter. She is interred in the city cemetery of Grenada near her husband and father.

Courtesy Isabel Wile Goldman, Shreveport, Louisiana

Meyer Wile was in the general merchandising business in Grenada. His descendants know nothing about his origin. It is known, however, that he belonged to the Grenada Masonic Lodge in 1855 and that his uncle, Simon Wile, enlisted

Courtesy Isabel Wile Goldman, Shreveport, Louisiana

in "Cap't Stanford's Co. L. Art'y, Miss." during the Civil War.

Meyer and his wife Isabella were very active in the community, according to the *Madison County Herald* in its 150th celebration issue. Meyer Wile died during the yellow fever epidemic in 1878 at the same time as did an uncle and also his wife's father, Joseph Streng.

CHARLESTON

Although Charleston was founded as early as 1837, it did not develop for many decades because there were no roads other than Indian trails. Community development was slow because of political conflicts.

At the turn of the century, however, a good road was built. Attracted by this and the timber in the area, a sawmill company came to settle in Charleston.

The Ben Weinstein family left Tunica, Mississippi, to make their home in Charleston. The Weinsteins joined the nearest Jewish congregation, which was in Cleveland sixty miles away.

Jake Weinstein, son of Ben and Rebecca Weinstein, was awarded the town's Outstanding Citizen award for 1937. Jake Weinstein, a merchant, was active in state politics and was a friend of many Mississippi governors, including Theodore Bilbo, the latter a friendship which his family could never understand.

Ben Weinstein, born in Budapest in 1859, left in 1880 for America. He often said that when he left Amsterdam, which was then a part of the German empire, the customs officials fleeced him of every penny he had saved. "When I came here, I had nothing. The first money I got in the United States was a coin which I found in the snow in New York. That was my lucky omen. The boat, I learned afterwards, sank on the way back."

He went to Memphis, Tennessee, where an older brother, Ben Weinstein, lived. It was there that he married Rebecca Friedman. In 1894, the Weinsteins came to Tunica, Mississippi, and then to Charleston at the turn of the century. Ben Weinstein died in Charleston in 1943.

Pictured here is Benjamin Weinstein at the age of sixty with his son, Max Weinstein, Sr., who was born in 1899.

Rebecca Friedman, born 1866, is pictured here at the age of twenty. She died in Charleston in 1914.

CLARKSDALE

Frequent floods from the Sunflower River and a disastrous fire retarded the growth of the town of Clarksdale, which was built at the intersection of two important Indian routes. By 1876 there was a small settlement of Jews of German descent. In the 1880s, a few Jews from Lithuania and from the east coast began to arrive, enough

Photographs courtesy Max Weinstein, Greenville

Photographs courtesy Mrs. A. W. Freyman, Greenville

76

to organize for services in 1894 in the home of Max Kaufman. In 1910 there were enough for a B'nai B'rith Lodge to be organized.

At the turn of the century, Herman Dansker, one of Clarksdale's leading citizens, founded a successful seed firm.

Temple Beth Israel was built at 69 Delta Avenue, and, according to the Clarksdale *Press Register*, "orthodox, conservative, and reform Jews found free expression in one house of worship." Rabbi A. H. Freyman, the congregation's first rabbi, stands behind the pulpit. The boys wearing prayer shawls [*taleisim*] are Abe Lipson at the left and Meyer Lipson at the right.

MARKS

Leopold Marks, after whom the town of Marks was named, realized the potential of the Coldwater River region when he bought a small trading boat and peddled goods up and down the river area. He opened his store and began to buy land.

Leopold Marks, Quitman County's first representative to the state legislature, served in that capacity for eight years.

When Leopold Marks, born 1851, left Germany to avoid conscription by the German army, he never dreamed that a town would be named for him. Landing in New York City in 1868, he knew no English and the only capital he had for getting started in business was the 18¢ that he had in his pocket. Later, he peddled jewelry across the county until he reached Friars Point, Mississippi.

He observed that the dense forests and the fer-

When Leopold Marks (born 1851) left Germany to avoid conscription by the German army, he never dreamed that a town would be named for him. Landing in New York City in 1868, he knew no English and the only capital he had for getting started in business was the 18¢ that he had in his pocket.

Photograph courtesy Rosalee Marks Goldstein, Atlanta, Georgia

tile banks of Cassidy's Bayou and of the Coldwater River had potential. He opened his store and began to buy land at 40¢ per acre.

Prejudice at first kept Leopold Marks from obtaining the land grant that he sought. He was shot at several times. He skirted the issue by forming the Marks Townsite Company and did manage to get the grant.

He encouraged the Yazoo and Mississippi Valley Railroad to come into the area by giving the railroad company, without cost, the right-of-way through his plantation plus ten acres of land.

Pauline, born in 1852, and he were married in 1875.

Photographs courtesy Rosalee Marks Goldstein, Atlanta, Georgia

North Central and Northeast Mississippi

OXFORD

It was the University of Mississippi that drew the brothers Hyman and Joseph Friedman, merchants, and their respective families to Oxford where their children might be able to obtain a fine education.

Joseph Friedman (1876–1959) and Bertha Wofsey (1879–1959) were married just before they came at the turn of the century to Oxford, where Friedman joined his brother, Hyman, in his business. Their daughter Rosalie, standing next to her father in the family photograph, married Jeff Leo Rubel of Okolona.

Photographs courtesy Rose (Rubel) Rich, New Orleans, Louisiana

PONTOTOC

When the Chickasaw Indians ceded their land in 1832, it included the large Indian settlement of Pontetok. The old village of Pontetok was abandoned when a new town, Pontotoc, was established in 1836.

Ellis and Minna Rauch had a store there where they sold dry goods. Other Jewish families in Pontotoc were the Bissingers, Wolfsons, Steppachers, and the Leon Gorden family.

Courtesy Rose (Rubel) Rich, New Orleans, Louisiana

Courtesy *Valhalla* yearbook, 1910

The 1910 graduation picture from the local high school annual shows Sara Rauch at far right and Eva Rauch, far left. Eva married Claude A. Titche, the son of Abraham and Ida (Levy) Titche of Port Gibson.

OKOLONA

The construction of the Mobile and Ohio Railroad in 1845 gave impetus to the growth of Okolona. The town grew quickly and became a big cotton market and by 1860 Okolona commanded the wagon trade of Chickasaw County. From Okolona, growers could ship their cotton to foreign ports.

When Julius Rubel opened his store in 1873, the town was a thriving business center.

The year 1948 marked the 75th anniversary of J. Rubel and Company. Descendants of Julius Rubel still operate the business in Okolona.

At age eighteen, Julius Rubel (1855–1932) left Kaiserlag, Germany, for the New World. On the boat coming to the United States he met his future wife, Rosa Morris. She went to her family

in South Carolina, and he traveled to Mississippi to join other Rubels who had preceded him. Eleven years later, Julius Rubel and Rosa Morris were married. Her mother and four sisters followed her to live in Okolona.

Members of the Rubel family are seen below. Standing, left to right, are Lotta Rubel (Cahn) and Gertrude Rubel (Wachtel). Seated, left to right, are Emanuel Rubel, Rosa Rubel, and Jeff Leo Rubel.

The three Rubel brothers are Julius of Okolona, Abe of Corinth, and Louis of Paducah, Kentucky.

The first store in Corinth, c. 1858, was established by Abe Rubel. According to *American Jewish Landmarks*, he raised funds to outfit the first company of volunteers from Corinth that joined the Confederate Army. His thirteen children had stores in Columbus, Aberdeen, West Point, and Corinth.

The valedictorian of the 1903 graduating class of the Okolona High School was Albert T. Mecklenburger, a native of Okolona born there in 1888.

He was the son of Dora (Feibelman), a native of Richmond, Virginia, and Marcus Mecklenburger who was born in Germany. Marcus started as a traveling salesman selling men's suits. The Mecklenburgers opened a general store in Okolona, selecting that town because it was a "railhead." Their daughter Effie (Mecklenburger) Greener was one of the first Jewish women to graduate, in 1909, from Mississippi State College for Women.

Albert T. Mecklenburger was a graduate of the University of Mississippi and the University of Chicago. He practiced law in Chicago. After a term as president of North Shore Congregation Israel, he went on to be president of the National Federation of Temple Brotherhoods.

The five Kaufman sisters. Back row, left to right: Lottie (Mrs. Leopold Loeb) of Columbus, Gertie (Mrs. Ike Simon) of Columbus; front row, left to right: Rosa (Mrs. Samuel Greenwald) of Meridian, Fannie (Mrs. Julius Loeb) of Columbus, Bettie (Mrs. Joe Meyer) of Meridian.

COLUMBUS

Until 1861 the people of Columbus fought the application of the M. & O. Railroad to secure right-of-way in the town, saying it would mar the landscape and bring undesirable people. During the Civil War, the Confederate government maintained a large arsenal in Columbus and, when Jackson fell, the seat of the government moved there. Simon Loeb came to Columbus during the Reconstruction days after the war. He was not, however, the first Jew to come to Columbus; reportedly, Jews had been in the city from as early as 1836.

Simon Loeb, born 1849 in Germany, left his native land and came to Columbus in 1867. After founding Simon Loeb & Company, he brought his brothers, Julius, Leopold, and Alexander (Alex), to America.

Even though he was busy with family responsibilities, building up a business, and innumer-

Courtesy Carolyn (Loeb) Leyens Meyer, Vicksburg

able community activities, he found time to be active in Congregation B'nai Israel (Hebrew: Children of Israel). The congregation, which had been formed in 1840, honored the patriarch of the Loeb family, who had served as a lay rabbi for many years, with an inscribed Bible.

Albert Loeb (1875–1945), the son of Simon and Lena Loeb, was born in Columbus. He re-

ceived a degree in agriculture and mechanics at the "A & M" college now called Mississippi State. In 1908 he married Edna Washer of Louisville, Kentucky. Albert Loeb joined Simon Loeb in the family business in Columbus.

STARKVILLE

In 1820 the Indians invited the missionaries to establish mission schools; these were probably the first agricultural and industrial schools in the South, according to James F. Brieger, author of *Hometown Mississippi*. Friends and relatives of the missionaries, as well as trappers and land speculators, moved in to begin the new city of Starkville.

In 1875, the entire business district of the town burned and then was rebuilt. It was during those years of intense growth that the Fried and Blumenfeld families came to Starkville to enter the mercantile business.

Their stately house on Jackson Street was built in 1880 by Simon and Sophie Fried. Members of the Fried-Blumenfeld family have occupied the house until recent times.

Simon Fried was born in 1843 in Ebelsbach, Bavaria, Germany, and came to the United States in 1857 at age fourteen. In 1868, he married Sophie Cramer, who was born in 1848 in Wilkes-Barre, Pennsylvania.

Shortly after the birth of their daughters Carrie (1869) and Nettie (1871), Simon Fried came to Starkville to be a junior partner in the mercantile firm of Blumenfeld-Fried, which operated until the mid-1950s. Their third daughter, Gussie, was born in Starkville in 1880.

Their daughter Carrie married the senior partner of the firm Bernhard Blumenfeld in 1888. Because there was no temple, their wedding took place at the Starkville Methodist Church, with a reception afterwards at the home of the bride's parents.

According to the *Starkville Daily News*, in an article by Shirley Carley, June 12, 1975:

> The house was surrounded by several acres . . .
> The grounds boasted two barns—one of which included a carriage house—, a trellised summer

house, two servant's cabins, a well house and grazing land for horses and cows.

The roomy interior of the house featured 12-foot ceilings, gleaming hardwood floors, nine handsome fireplaces, and a beautiful carved staircase leading from the large entry hall to the second floor. On the main floor were a parlor, a card room, dining room, library, two bedrooms and baths, kitchen, pantry and butler's pantry. Off the large upstairs hall were five bedrooms and two baths and a trunk room. There were outside stairs leading from the rear of the house up to this floor. . . .

Religious services for the small Jewish community were held in the Odd Fellows Building. The Frieds and Blumenfelds were integral parts of the Starkville community as well as leaders in their small Jewish congregation.

WINONA

Among the Jews who came to Winona were the Samson Wiener (see Canton) and the Julius Harris families. The Wiener family came there in the 1860s and later moved to Canton. The Harris family came to Winona in 1880.

Theresa Peavy was born in 1838 in Poland.

Courtesy Minna Harris Smith, Monroe, Louisiana

She married Julius H. Harris, and they had three children: Ansel Meyer, born 1857; Charles, born 1859; and Rosa, born 1863. Both Julius and Theresa Harris are interred in Canton's Jewish cemetery.

Courtesy Minna Harris Smith, Monroe, Louisiana

Julius H. Harris is shown sitting on the porch of his house on Montgomery Street in Winona. The Polish-born Julius married Theresa Peavy in Boston in 1856 and moved to Bath, Maine. The couple eventually moved south with their three children to Friars Point, Mississippi. Their last move was to Winona in the late 1870s. Mr. Harris died in 1907.

Yetta Weiner was born in Canton in 1867, the daughter of Caroline and Samson Wiener. She married Ansel Meyer Harris, who was born in Bath, Maine, in 1857, son of Julius and Theresa Harris, who later moved to Winona. The wedding took place in the groom's home in 1890.

Courtesy Minna Harris Smith, Monroe, Louisiana

84

MACON

The Choctaw Indians ceded land to the government when the Treaty of Dancing Rabbit Creek was signed in Noxubee County. The earliest known Jew in that semi-frontier county was Chapman Levy, a lawyer-politician, who engaged in correspondence in 1836 with President Martin Van Buren when the latter was standard-bearer of the Democratic Party.

The home of the Jacob Holberg family in Macon became known as the "Old Holberg Place."

Courtesy Ralph G. Holberg, Jr., Mobile, Alabama

Holberg left Germany at the age of nineteen and began life in America as a peddler. In 1857 he opened a small store in Macon. Four years later he enlisted in Company G, 1st Regiment (cavalry). After four years of service in the Confederate Army, he returned to Macon in 1865 to marry and to continue his business. An article by John A. Tyson written in 1894 in an unidentified Noxubee County paper eulogizes Jacob Holberg as "a splendid citizen . . . most charitable, benevolent man. . . ." Tyson concludes, "If he was not a converted Jew, he showed by his life and conduct that he was a Christ-like one."

SHUQUALAK

The town of Shuqualak, founded in 1857, grew up around farming and lumbering activities.

Julius Yaretzky came from Lauderdale to Shuqualak, where he dealt in scrap metal, hides, and animal bones. Both the Marks and Yaretzky families were close enough to Meridian to take part in religious services and bury their dead in Temple Beth Israel's cemetery.

After his release as a Confederate prisoner of war, Polish-born Julius Yaretzsky came back to the South. He went to Lauderdale, Mississippi, where he had met Dora (Buck) Lowenstein (1848–1891) during the war.

Brooklyn-born Dora Buck and her brother Isaac came to the South when their father remarried. The children were given away to be adopted, because, as told in the words of Julius Yaretzky, "the stepmother was not agreeable to the children." Isaac went to the Newmans of Mobile, where he died of yellow fever. Dora went to the childless J. Lowensteins of Lauderdale.

After the marriage of Julius Yaretzky and Dora (Buck) Lowenstein, Yaretzsky went into partnership with his brother Marx and with Mr. Newman, who had adopted his wife's brother. The partners eventually left; Julius remained in Shuqualak.

When Mrs. Yaretzky died in 1891, her husband sent two of their five children, Frank and

When Mrs. Yaretzky died in 1891, her husband sent two of their five children, Frank and Richard, to Bellfaire, the B'nai B'rith-sponsored orphan home in Cleveland, Ohio. The father sent them there hoping that they would have an opportunity for a better education and life than he could give them in the little village.

Richard, to Bellfaire, the B'nai B'rith-sponsored orphan home in Cleveland, Ohio. The father sent them there hoping that they would have an opportunity for a better education and life than he could give them in the little village.

A resentful Frank did not communicate with his family for approximately five years. Beginning in 1896, however, he wrote several times. One letter requested information about his family background. Another letter was written possibly because the teenager was studying Civil War history. In it he asked about relics that his father might have saved from his war-time weaponry. Julius Yaretzky's touching attempts in three letters to share his life and thoughts, hoping to bridge the years spent in estrangement, never resolved the tension. One letter can be found in the introduction to this book.

Julius Yaretzky, who served as the mayor of Shuqualak for several terms, is seen here in his regalia as he served as Tyler of the state Grand Lodge of Masons.

Courtesy Mrs. A. W. Freyman, Greenville

KOSCIUSKO

After many changes, the name of Kosciusko, after the Polish hero of the American Revolution, was chosen as the permanent name for this central Mississippi town. In order to establish a library, stock was sold at $10 a share. Two boarding schools, one for boys and one for girls, had been established in 1845. The schools and the lumbering in the region attracted some settlers.

Among the early Jewish settlers was the Isaac Simon family. Fredal Marx came to the United States in the 1840s, and she married Henry Harrison Thal of Kosciusko. Their daughter Elisa was born there in 1851. Joseph Meyer, the son of Jacob and Henrietta (Weil) Meyer, was born in that town in 1862. Shortly afterwards, Jacob Meyer packed his family and household goods in a wagon and moved to Marion and then again to Meridian.

Isaac Simon (1835–1888), born in Rhine, Prussia, lived in Louisiana when he first came to the United States. After joining the Confederate Army in Memphis, he received a stomach wound in battle, which left him in poor health the rest of his life.

He and his wife Marie settled in Kosciusko, where they had either a hotel or a boarding house. One daughter, Claire (Simon) Lowenberg, remained in Kosciusko.

PHILADELPHIA

A large old Choctaw Indian town was the site upon which Philadelphia was built in Neshoba County. The cost of the land was originally 75¢ per acre. Philadelphia adjoins the large Pearl River Indian Reservation, which still serves as a home for many Choctaw Indians.

Rumors that a railroad would be built with Philadelphia on its route began in 1895. The railroad began operation in 1905 at the same time that David Kasdan, a peddler, opened his store in Philadelphia where whites, blacks, and Indians shopped.

"On the following Monday I started out for the country with a pack of 75 pounds on my back. The country homes in those days weren't as thick as today. They were sometimes two and three miles apart. The sunny South was really sunny and plenty hot."

Three soldiers in the Czar's army, c. 1902–1903, left to right: Sam Cohen, David Kasdan, his uncle, seated; and Chiamnev Gurevitch, another nephew of Kasdan.

David, the son of Joseph Chyem Kasdan, wrote a memoir about life in Russia, conscription into the Czar's Army in 1896, and his life in America.

He accepted the invitation of his nephew, Sam Cohen, to come to Kosciusko. He wrote, "I decided to emigrate to a new America—Mississippi." His memoir includes a sensitive account of his start as a peddler. When he arrived in Kosciusko he found a fellow countryman by the name of Raskind: "He could not read or write Russian and here he was a big-shot already with a store. I thought to myself that if a man like him could work himself up to such a thing as having a store, then how could I miss it. . . ."

It wasn't so easy: "On the following Monday I started out for the country with a pack of 75 pounds on my back. The country homes in those days weren't as thick as today. They were sometimes two and three miles apart. The sunny South was really sunny and plenty hot."

As Kasdan developed rapport with his customers and gave requests his special attention, he graduated to a horse and wagon, to be paid for "on time," and made his first ten dollar sale.

He wrote of his attraction to Annie Epstein of Kosciusko; as a poor peddler, he was not in a position to woo her. She moved with her family to Louisville, Kentucky. The hard-working peddler saved sufficient money to open a store in Philadelphia and then to go to Louisville to court "my Mrs. Kasdan," as he later respectfully referred to her.

Successful in business and in personal life, David Kasdan wrote his memoirs at the age of seventy-five.

DeKALB

There were few Jews in Kemper County.

Jacob Jonas, an early resident, served as postmaster of Sucarnochee from 1871 until World War I.

Joe Cramer and Marx Rosenbaum, who started as itinerant peddlers, are on record as Jews who lived in Scooba.

One of the most prominent citizens who lived in the county was Charles Rosenbaum of De-Kalb. He was born in Wahalak in the northeast part of the county (no longer on current maps) in 1845. He was the son of Carolyn and Marx

Rosenbaum and remained a bachelor all his life. He helped to organize the Union Bank and Trust of DeKalb. When he died in 1932, among the many honorary pallbearers at his funeral was John Stennis, later to become the United States Senator from Mississippi.

Among those who are memorialized by inscriptions on the Confederate monument in the DeKalb town square are Aron and Jacob Rosenbaum who "are probably buried in Civil War cemeteries or on battlefields somewhere." They were the sons of Carolyn and Marx Rosenbaum.

Meridian

THE Meridian Jewish story actually began at Marion, a heavily wooded town six miles from the center of Meridian. Marion boasted the Marion Academy, which was built in 1837 and was the first school in Lauderdale County. Mississippi land records show that David Rosenbaum purchased a lot in Marion in 1837.

According to a study of the *Lauderdale Republican* made by Fred W. Edmiston of issues 1854 to 1856, other Jewish families attracted to Marion were those of Abraham Dreyfus (the German later Anglicized to Threefoot), Isaac Rosenbaum, Leopold Rosenbaum, and E. Lowenstein. Jacob Cohen placed an advertisement for a lost pony. In addition, Jacob Meyer and his family moved there from Kosciusko. Many of these families remained in Marion during the Civil War when Federal troops scoured the town for food.

Six miles away, Jewish families had begun to arrive in Meridian to join those who had gradually moved out of Marion to Meridian. The railroad missed Marion by two miles and the town began to wither. The final blow to Marion came when the county seat was moved to Meridian. The little mud-streeted village of Meridian, comprising 1⅛ miles and fifteen families in 1860, grew to become a railroad center. By 1869, a congregation of ten Reform Jewish families were meeting in a small school house at Ninth Street and Twenty-fourth Avenue in Meridian.

Plans had been laid jointly by the Jews of both Marion and Meridian to build a common house of worship midway between the two towns. Meanwhile, two itinerant peddlers died in Meridian and Meridian Jews bought land to begin a Jewish cemetery. Despite the protest of Marion Jews, the Jewish center had shifted to Meridian.

On February 16, 1864, when Union troops en-

" . . . to our greatest astonishment and delightful surprise, we beheld a magnificent structure, a gorgeous temple, which indeed in beauty, neatness and elegance equals to many that we have seen in larger cities. It is the only building in the city which is lighted by gas (manufactured in the rear of the temple) and which adds a great deal to the attraction of the building."

tered Meridian, General W. T. Sherman ordered that the railroad tracks and all items of possible value to the Confederate forces be destroyed. After the city was sacked, it was set afire.

The townspeople rebuilt, but the yellow fever in 1878 reduced the population even as the people prayed for an early frost to quell the epidemic. Even the tornado of 1906 did not impede the growth of Meridian as a railroad center. The city directory of 1884 declared: "Twelve passenger trains and over twenty freight trains arrive at and leave Meridian daily." According to the *Meridian Star*, the city in 1880 ranked fourth among the cities of the state and climbed to first place in 1910, where it remained until the 1920s.

By 1879, Congregation Beth Israel's fifty members had erected the house of worship shown in this architect's sketch. I. Marks was the president of the congregation at that time. In the book *Reflections of Southern Jewry*, Charles Wessolowsky reports in a letter on a visit to Meridian that year:

> . . . to our greatest astonishment and delightful surprise, we beheld a magnificent structure, a gorgeous temple, which indeed in beauty, neatness and elegance equals to many that we have seen in larger cities. It is the only building in the city which is lighted by gas (manufactured in the rear of the temple) and which adds a great deal to the attraction of the building.

The Jewish South (New Orleans, 1879) reports that there were thirty-two children in the Sabbath School. The Reverend W. Weinstein, L. Solomon, and Leon Lowi served as teachers.

An oldtimer reported that brides and confirmands used his family home across the street for last minute primping. They walked across Twenty-second Avenue on a red carpet laid down especially for them over the dirt street to enter Temple Beth Israel's sanctuary illuminated for the occasion by its thirty gas lights.

In sharp contrast to its previous house of worship, the second temple of Congregation Beth Israel, built in 1906 at Eleventh Street and Twenty-fourth Avenue, was Grecian style.

Confirmation Class, 1895, Temple Beth Israel. Standing, left to right: Carrye Rosenbaum, Rabbi Wolff Wilner, Carrie Netter. Sitting, left to right: Amelia Greenwald, Adolph Weil, Eva Holtz

The European House was very likely the first Meridian hotel. Charles Wessolowsky wrote about it in 1879: "In the morning we departed for Meridian, Mississippi, where we landed in due time and were greeted by the shout of hotel drummers, soliciting customers for their respective hotels. Being an entire stranger in the city and not knowing what hotel to make our headquarters, we followed one who brought us to the European House, F. Weitman, proprietor, and indeed we were pleased with our accidental solicitor."(F. Weitman was a member of the Jewish community.)

Going down the right side of the street, one can see the following: the Rosenbaum building, the Arky building, the Winner and Meyer building, and the Meyer Brothers farm implement location. Coming back up the other side of the street and moving to the left one sees the Marks-Rothenberg Company department store, the entrance to the Grand Opera House, and, at the left edge of the picture, the First National Bank, where several Jews served on its board of directors.

Israel Marks was born in Germany and came here through the port of New Orleans in 1856. He worked his way as far as Alexandria, Louisiana. When the Civil War broke out, he joined Boone's Battery.

After the war, Israel Marks peddled until 1870, when he came with Mr. Lichtenstein to Meridian. Tax records show their wholesale-retail general merchandise store, called Marks-Lichtenstein, was opened at Sowashee Station on what was called Front Street because it fronted the railroad station. The last tax record of the combined business of Marks-Lichtenstein was in 1883.

Marks, Lichtenstein and Company, architect's sketch.
Courtesy Meridian Public Library, Mississippi Room Collection.

Israel Marks was the only son of the first marriage of Sara (Sugarman) Marks. Her second marriage to Sam Rothenberg gave Israel Marks three half-brothers and two sisters.

The four brothers—Israel Marks, and Levi, Sam, and Marks Rothenberg—went into business together using the name, "Marks, Rothenberg and Company." The building remains a Meridian landmark.

The Fair and Exposition Corporation, composed of I. Marks, the three Rothenberg brothers, the Threefoot brothers, W. Rosenbaum, and three non-Jews, gave all of the corporation's acreage to the city to be used as a park, later known as Highland Park.

I. Marks was honored for his work as president of the commissioners of Highland Park with a statue placed in a position of prominence.

The Fair and Exposition Corporation, composed of I. Marks, the three Rothenberg brothers, the Threefoot brothers, W. Rosenbaum, and three non-Jews, gave all of the corporation's acreage to the city to be used as a park, later known as Highland Park. I. Marks was honored for his work as president of the commissioners of Highland Park with a statue placed in a position of prominence.

Photograph by Cecil Adkins, Meridian

Marks, Rothenberg and Company moved in 1899 from their Front Street location into their new building at Fifth Street and Twenty-second Avenue. Note the archways through which a lady's carriage could enter a 25 x 40 feet open courtyard.

Cautious though enterprising, the firm planned a building that would house their grocery and general merchandise business but that could readily be converted, if needed during the city's hey-day as a railroad center, into a hotel. The many windows were placed judiciously to allow for hotel room partitions.

Not long after, annual sales amounted to one and a half million dollars.

Israel Marks and family. Front row: Hettye (mother), I. Marks (father), Simon; back row: Edward, Annie, Arthur, Sara

93

Four female generations of one family. They are, left to right, Annie Ritterman, great grandmother; Annie (Marks) Baum (1870–1946), mother; Hettye H. Marks (1850–1912), grandmother; and little Rebecca Julia Baum, who married Lewis Sonnetheil. Picture taken c. 1895.

Grateful for their business success in Meridian, the four partners of the Marks, Rothenberg and Company department store sought to share their good fortune in the New World with their fellow citizens by building in 1890 the Grand Opera House, adjacent to their business.

Grand Opera House, interior.
Courtesy Meridian Public Library, Mississippi Room Collection.

The first presentation was Johann Strauss's opera, *The Gypsy Baron,* which opened on December 17, 1890. It was backed by twenty-five full sets of scenery painted by Sossman and Landes of Chicago.

Grateful for their business success in Meridian, the four partners of the Marks, Rothenberg and Company department store sought to share their good fortune in the New World with their fellow citizens by building in 1890, the Grand Opera House, adjacent to their business.

This non-profit venture brought first-class actors and musicians to Meridian. The great Enrico Caruso, Al F. Fields Minstrels, Frederick Warde in *Hamlet,* the Cincinnati Symphony Orchestra, among others, brought audiences from all over the South.

During the intermission, tea and cakes were served to guests at their seats, if ordered in advance. A box of chocolates from Netters was a "must" gift from the men to their ladies.

The *New York Dramatic Mirror,* in 1891, reported: "Good companies invariably draw full houses and . . . Meridian is the city in the South for theatrical companies."

Arthur J. Lyons was born to a poor family in Mobile, Alabama, in 1872. He came to Meridian at age twenty. In 1901 he married Josie Rosenbaum of Meridian.

After the 1906 tornado almost destroyed the center of town, the Lyons Brothers Company bought and renovated the damaged Baum block. This huge warehouse along the railroad track

Courtesy *Illustrated Handbook of Meridian, Mississippi,* 1907

facilitated the rapid handling of fresh fruit from Florida plus carloads of cotton, grain, and hay.

Lyons Brothers advertised that they were "sole agents for the celebrated Hopfen Weis, a pure non-alcoholic drink recommended by all physicians as a healthful tonic."

Arthur Lyons served as the president of Temple Beth Israel for four years, 1917–1921. He gave a building as a gift to the Tuberculosis Sanitorium.

Mr. and Mrs. A. J. Lyons opened their home on the corner of Seventh Street and 26th Avenue to music lovers of Meridian to raise money for war sufferers. Mr. Lyon, often called "an artist on the violin," gave a concert.

The dining room and residence of Mr. and Mrs. Levi Rothenberg.

Built c. 1880, the home of Leopold Rosenbaum was at Seventh Street and 27th Avenue.

Joseph Baum & Son, wholesale and retail dealers in dry goods, clothing, and plantation supplies, were housed in the "Baum Block" on Twenty-fifth Avenue, extending from Second to Third streets. Their advertisement in the 1882 city directory proclaimed that they were "Agents for DuPont's Gun Powder and Agents for the Ziegler Shoe." The cost of the Baum block was $25,000.

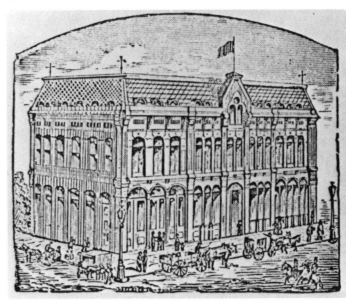

Boosen, Prussia, was the birthplace of Joseph Baum, 1844–1905. In 1869 he had a dry goods store in Meridian. The older daughter of the Baum family pictured here is Nettie Baum.

Rebecca "Bookie" Feltenstein, the daughter of Nettie and Sam Meyer.

Jacob Meyer (1832–1900), born in Neuweid, Germany, married Henrietta (Weil) Meyer (1835–1870) who was born in Engenheim, Bavaria. The family came first to Kosciusko, then to Marion, settling finally in Meridian, where descendants still reside.

Meyer Brothers, a firm headed by the sons of Jacob and Henrietta, was a large wholesale grocery company. In addition, the firm had a livery stable and built the Lamar Hotel.

Joe Meyer and his wife Bettie Kaufman Meyer (1868–1931). Their handsome Victorian style house built in 1890 was at the corner of Harris Street and Thirtieth Avenue.

Joe Meyer bequeathed money to the synagogues and to almost every church of his beloved city. The Lauderdale Girl Scout Camp is on forty acres that he gave specifically for that purpose.

Nettie (Baum) Meyer (1868–1931), the daughter of Joseph Baum, married a Meridian businessman, Sam Meyer.

Joe Meyer

Bettie Kaufman Meyer

Mollie (Leinkauf) Kaufman, Mobile, Alabama, is surrounded here by her Meridian grandchildren. Mrs. Herman Kaufman (1837–1906) was born in Pressburgh, Hungary.

Standing in the rear, left to right, are Harold Meyer and Helen Meyer. In the second row, left to right, are Herbert Greenwald and Irma (later Eichold) Greenwald. Seated on grandmother's lap is Irving Greenwald and kneeling next to him is Lucille Greenwald (later Metzger).

Seated in front, left to right, are Joe M. Greenwald and Sam Greenwald; back, left to right, are Joe Greenwald and Sam Meyer.

According to 1837 land records, David Rosenbaum (1820–1892) purchased a lot at age seventeen in Marion. He came from Schossenreich,

Bavaria, to Marion, where he joined Isaac Rosenbaum to form the business partnership of D. & I. Rosenbaum.

He went to Columbus, Mississippi, to enlist in the Confederate Army but was excused for reasons of health.

When Meridian became a railroad center, he moved there and established D. Rosenbaum & Sons and sold merchandise. He was the vice president of Congregation Beth Israel when its first temple was built and served afterwards as its president for nine years.

Caroline Rosenbaum

Descendants of David and Caroline (Koch) Rosenbaum (1829–1897) still laugh over the story that tells how she outwitted Union Army soldiers.

Word reached Mrs. Rosenbaum that soldiers were confiscating all available food and carting it off from Marion. The strong-willed woman put some of her children in one bed and lit the wood-burning fireplace to get the room and the children warm. She quickly shoved all available food supplies and valuables under the bed. Shortly before the knock came at the door, she artfully put a few red blotches on the children's warm faces. When Caroline Rosenbaum seemingly apologetically ushered the soldiers into the room, they took one horrified look at the flushed and spotted faces and left—abruptly!

Lewis Rosenbaum (1859–1898) was born in Marion the son of Caroline and David Rosenbaum. He became the first chief of the Meridian Volunteer Fire Department and was instrumental in putting it on a pay basis. When Cornelia Metzger, his first wife, died, he married Adele Weil of Meridian.

Alex Loeb was the first Loeb in Meridian, brought to the United States from Germany by his brother, Simon Loeb, who preceded him in Columbus. Alex Loeb married Mollie Threefoot of Meridian.

The Alex Loeb store, organized in 1887, originally stood in the Rosenbaum Building, as seen below, before the move to its location on the site of what was originally the Meyer Brothers farm implement store on Twenty-fifth Street.

An ardent and faithful Jew, he served as president of Temple Beth Israel and was called upon frequently to conduct services.

Lewis Rosenbaum.

A marble plaque in the corridor of Wechsler School tells the story of Rabbi Judah Wechsler, who was the spiritual leader of Congregation Beth Israel from 1887 to 1893.

WECHSLER SCHOOL
THIS ORIGINAL BUILDING WAS ERECTED IN 1888 BEING THE FIRST BRICK PUBLIC SCHOOL BUILDING IN MISSISSIPPI FOR NEGRO CHILDREN AND WAS PAID FOR FROM THE PROCEEDS OF A BOND ISSUE VOTED BY THE WHITE CITIZENS OF MERIDIAN. IT WAS NAMED FOR RABBI WECHSLER ON REQUEST OF THE NEGROES OF MERIDIAN BECAUSE HE LED THE MOVEMENT TO PROVIDE PUBLIC SCHOOL FACILITIES FOR THEIR CHILDREN.

Photographs courtesy A. L. Cahn, Meridian

An article in the Meridian newspaper in 1910 about the death of pioneer settler, L. Rosenbaum, stated that "'Uncle Abe', as he was familiarly called, came to Meridian when it was in its infancy and nursed it from the weakling village it was to the strong and populous city of today."

Abraham Leon Rosenbaum (1848–1910) was the son of Caroline and Marx Rosenbaum of DeKalb. He came to Meridian in 1866. An 1885 Sanborn map places his first business on Front Street. The Rosenbaum Building shown here still stands in downtown Meridian.

Flora Rosenbaum, wife of A. L. Rosenbaum (1861–1916).

The residence of A. L. and Flora Rosenbaum at Fourteenth Street and Twenty-third Avenue.

Richeldorf of Kuhr Hessen in Germany was the birthplace of Abraham Dreyfus (1824–1898). "Dreyfus" translates from the German to "Threefoot," which became the family name in the United States.

During the war, Abraham Threefoot made shoes for the Confederate Army. His wife, Tarris

(Levy) Threefoot (1830–1888), always spoke of Union soldiers as "damn Yankees," because they knocked down her picket fence at the Threefoot home in Marion.

The family moved to Meridian where the Threefoot name stood for fine quality in saddles

and harnesses (shop shown above). The Threefoot sons expanded the business into other areas (building shown below).

Abraham Threefoot, seated center, with his family.

101

Kutcher Threefoot (1861–1924) born in Marion, Mississippi, was the son of Abraham and Tarris (Levy) Threefoot. "K," as he was called, married Julia Rothenberg (1864–1950), a sister of the Marks-Rothenberg brothers, in 1887.

This picture of Kutcher "K" Threefoot, which hangs in the administrative office building of the Meridian public school system, serves as a reminder of his years of service as president of the Board of Education.

Courtesy Dr. Kenneth Loflin, Superintendent of Public Schools, Meridian

The home of Julia and Kutcher Threefoot was at Twenty-second Avenue and Thirteenth Street.

Photograph by Carol Perkins, *The Meridian Star*

Courtesy *Meridian Illustrated*, 1904.

Julius Elson (1841–1907) is listed in early city directories as a merchant. He married Dora Neubauer (1853–1935). Their sixteen-room Victorian home, built on the corner of Eleventh Street and 29th Avenue in 1895, was filled with carefully crafted items that made it a showplace.

Most Jews came to the New World to escape poverty, among other reasons. Mark Winner (1838–1910), however, was an exception to the rule. In 1853, the Winners, a family of means, left Posen, Germany, to make a new start in Milano, Texas.

Young Winner served in Captain David Pierson's Company C., Winn Rifles, Third Louisiana

Infantry. He used to quip that he "seemed to be the only soldier who remained a private after the war. All the Confederate soldiers he met were Captains, Majors, or Colonels."

Mark and Hannah (Newman) Winner came to Meridian in 1872 and built a temporary home where Weidman's restaurant now stands.

Mark Winner and Jacob Meyer founded Winner & Meyer Co., the forerunner of Winner and Klein department store pictured here, which stood at Fourth Street and 22nd Avenue.

Winner and Klein department store

Courtesy Meridian Public Library, Mississippi Room Collection

Mark Winner's elaborate gravestone in the Beth Israel cemetery in Meridian is a rarity, per-

Mark Winner's elaborate gravestone in the Beth Israel cemetery in Meridian is a rarity, perhaps because one of the Ten Commandments opposed idolatry: "Thou shalt not make unto thee a graven image . . ." (Exodus 20:4ff).

haps because one of the Ten Commandments opposed idolatry: "Thou shalt not make unto thee a graven image . . ." (Exodus 20:4ff).

The children of Mark and Hannah Winner. Leo Winner is standing; Sara Winner (later Meyer) is holding a purse; and Pauline Winner (later Klein) is holding a doll.

Courtesy Clarice (Klein) Rosenbaum Ullman, Meridian

103

Judge Abe Klein   Courtesy *The Jewish Ledger, 1923*.

Photographs courtesy Clarice (Klein) Rosenbaum Ullman, Meridian

Judge Abe Klein (1841–1934) served in an Alabama regiment. An inscription on his gravestone reads: "A loyal son of the Confederacy." He married Fannie Jacoby (1847–1930) of Mobile, Alabama. Abe Klein served as president of Temple Beth Israel for many years.

His son, Simon Klein (1877–1965), pictured dressed for his confirmation at Temple Beth Israel, was born in Lauderdale. He married Pauline Winner. An excellent businessman, he was a significant factor in the expansion of the firm of Winner and Klein.

The St. Louis Junk Company was founded by Lewis Davidson (1876–1946) who is seen (right) walking to his business. This was the humble be-

Courtesy Frances Davidson, Meridian

ginning of the Southern Pipe and Supply Company, which was built by his sons and a grandson into a large company with branches in many parts of the South.

Many Friday mornings he would go with his horse and wagon to Shuqualak to do a little business and to visit with his friend Julius Yaretzky, who dealt in junk, hides, and animal bones. After their business was completed and after some conversation in Yiddish, they would stop at the local barber's for a haircut.

He worshipped with the small orthodox congregation, Ohel Jacob (Hebrew: the Tent of Jacob), which was begun in 1880.

When Harry Strauss moved from Jackson to be near his daughter Sadie (Strauss) Lerner, he and his son-in-law, William Lerner (born 1884) opened Strauss and Lerner Jewelry store.

Leah (Zeman) (1873–1962) and Wolfe Wigransky (1864–1929) came to Meridian from Columbia, Mississippi, in 1893. The family name in Lozdijai, Lithuania, was Vigransky. In their first store on Fifth Street and Twenty-fifth Avenue, their ladies' apparel business was downstairs and the family lived upstairs. Wolfe Wigransky liked his side-line business even better than the retail business. The grown grandchildren still maintain that "Grampa Wiggs" was the best storyteller ever.

One of their daughters, Gertrude (Wigransky) Berman was an achiever even as a child when she won a state-wide spelling bee. The "spelldown" word was *onomatopoeia*. In her role in a movie made in Meridian in 1917, shown below, she is surrounded by curious onlookers. Her favorite role was the lead in Marc Connelly's play, *The Green Pastures*. Under her professional name, Jessica Lee, she had the honor of performing before President Franklin D. Roosevelt at the White House.

105

Paula Ackerman, Meridian, was the first woman in the United States* invited by an established congregation to serve as its rabbi. When

Amelia Greenwald

*"The only precedent in the entire long history of Judaism, here and abroad, was that for nineteen years an English Jewess, Mrs. Lilly Montague, had served as the spiritual head of a Reform temple in London."

Jews, Justice and Judaism, Robert St. John; Garden City, N.Y., 1969.

her husband, the rabbi of Temple Beth Israel, died after serving the congregation for twenty-six years, the members called upon her at age sixty-four to succeed him.

In an interview for the *New York World Telegram and Sun,* she revealed that she would begin work at 5:30 a.m. and not finish until late at night. People who were traveling through the state would make it a point to attend services conducted by her. Some came to scoff, but many left inspired and impressed.

As the wife of a rabbi and as acting rabbi, she was active in local, state, and national sisterhood groups. She served as a member for more than a decade on the national synagogue committee of the Union of American Hebrew Congregations.

Her unique position brought her world acclaim. She is mentioned in source books such as *Who's Who of American Women,* the 1966 *International Biography,* and in Robert St. John's book, *Jews, Justice and Judaism.* At age fifty-five she was counted as one of "Ten Outstanding Jewish Women" for that year. On her ninetieth birthday, Mrs. Ackerman was honored by the Central Conference of American Rabbis at a public gathering.

Hailed in the *Paris Times* of January 9, 1927, as ". . . a 'born nurse,' an organizer, and a leader of women,"Amelia Greenwald deserves her place in history along with Florence Nightingale and Clara Barton.

During World War I, she saw service with the American Expeditionary Force as chief nurse in several evacuation hospitals and, after the signing of the Armistice, she accompanied the First Army of Occupation to Germany to establish its first hospital in Coblenz.

Following the war, she was instrumental in establishing Poland's first school of nursing which was at the Jewish Hospital and her work was acclaimed by the *Paris Times.* According to the *Palestine Post,* December 18, 1912, Miss Greenwald "was publicly decorated by President Moscicki with the Golden Cross of merit, the first woman to receive that decoration."

Her gravestone in the Beth El cemetery in Meridian bears the simple inscription: "Nurse, Army Nurse Corps, World War I." Her name was recently entered in the records of Women in Military Service for America and of the Jewish War Veterans.

Central Mississippi

McCOMB

In 1872 when Colonel H. S. McComb, president of the New Orleans, Jackson & Great Northern Railroad, moved the company headquarters from New Orleans to a place called Elizabethtown, the town's name was changed to McComb. A sawmill was established in the town in 1873, and a small number of Jewish merchants came into McComb; the town grew around the economy of the railroad and the sawmill. The Jews went to the nearby town of Summit for their religious needs.

A. Heidenreich was born in Riga, Russia, in 1835. The inscription on his tombstone in the Summit Jewish cemetery tells that "he died in McComb City, Feb. 20, 1895." Identified in front of his business are, at left, Henry, Ben, and Mrs. A. Heidenreich.

Courtesy *The McComb Enterprise Journal*

SUMMIT

The first record of a Jew in Pike County is a license to peddle, granted in 1848 to Samuel Isaacs.

Long before the railroad came to Summit in 1856, there were Jewish residents among the first settlers. What had been a village of about two hundred persons, with no churches or schools and only four stores, two of which were owned by Jews, became the largest town in Pike County. Captain T. Gracey records: "The first store building . . . was that of Louis Alcus and Isaac Scherck, his nephew, who were second to none in contributing to the building up of the town." Other pioneer merchants were Sol Hyman and his brother, Sam, who had a store south of Meadville Street.

The Jews of Summit organized in 1870 as Congregation Ohaveh Shalom (Hebrew: Lovers of

Peace). Soon afterwards they built a synagogue on Baldwin Street. Records of the deed were destroyed in a courthouse fire in 1882. The tornado of 1924 destroyed the building. None of the original families remained in Summit.

Jews who settled in towns and villages in Amite and Pike counties near Summit. [Sources: *The Summit Sun* 1940, 1945, 1958; *History of Pike County;* Mrs. John C. Covington, *Source Records*, Pike County.]

Liberty. Abram Hiller sold his mercantile business here in 1852 to settle in Summit.

Kahnville was named for a Jewish merchant by the name of Louis Kahn who is buried in the Summit cemetery. He died in 1891.

Magnolia. From marriage notices in the *Magnolia Gazette*: "3/25/1881, Hiller/Levy, md. in Magnolia at Jonas Hiller's res., Sun. 3/20/1881, by Rev. J. L. Lencht [Leucht?] of N. O., Daniel Hiller of Canton, Miss., and Julia Levy of Bastrop, La."

Osyka. Captain T. Gracey reminisces in the *Sun*: "Osyka was a thriving place of about 1500 inhabitants, loading and unloading daily from ten to fifteen cars. Principal merchants . . . Lewis Alcus. . . ."

Holmesville. From *Source Records*: "Early in the forties John D. Jacobowsky came in from Prussia, settled in Holmesville and opened a mercantile business, being associated with Joseph Hart, who married his sister, Susan, and later on with Jake Hart, his nephew, who married Pauline Hilborn, sister to Ben Hilborn.

Pincus Morris, Mike, Mary, Sarah, Hannah, and Bertha were children of Joe Hart and Susan Jacobowsky.

Hyman, Meyer, Isaac and Simon Lichtenstein were residents of Holmesville and occupied a store on the corner opposite that of Jacobowsky and Hart, the latter being on the same block and connected with the hotel building. . . .

Dorothy Carrol Rayan described the cemetery and its ethereal quality:

On a peaceful, shady hilltop on the North Eastern perimeter of the town is the Summit Jewish Cemetery, accessible only by a narrow gravel road,

the fight to keep the premises clean and neat is a never ending one.

Here are buried a number of the true pioneers of the infancy and early days of Summit. The ancient tombstones, some with symbols of an abiding faith, many lettered in old Hebrew, recall such familiar names to native Summitonians as Heidenreich, Kiersky, Levy, Moyse, Hiller and others.

The Jewish cemetery is a historic bit of land . . . the final resting place of many of the builders of our town.

(D.A.R., Genealogical Records Committee, Judith Robinson Chapter, McComb)

The small Jewish community in Summit answered the call to serve the Confederate cause in proportionately large numbers. The following list is a composite of names listed in the *Summit Sun* and of inscriptions on cemetery stones.

Louis Aronson	Nathan Hart
Jule Block	Pincus Hart
Sol Block	Charles Levy
Ben Forscheimer	Emanuel Levy
Ben Hilborn	Charles Mendelson
Hertz (Hatch) Hiller	A. Moak
Nathan Hiller	Isadore Moyse
Sam Hyman	Isaac Scherck
Jacob Hart	Louis Scherck
Morris Hart	

Although all of these men survived the war, many of them were eventually laid to rest in this historic cemetery.

The well-constructed house of Isadore and Rosalie (Moak) Moyse still stands in Summit.

Isadore Moyse (1838–1887), born in Portigny, Alsace-Lorraine, was a pioneer merchant in Pike County. He came to Summit with his wife Rosalie (1839–1915) who was also born in Alsace-Lorraine.

Isadore Moyse saw service as a private in the Confederate military. He was a master of the Summit lodge of Masons 1868–1869 and a director of the Peabody Public School.

The family name, Moyse or Moise, is Spanish for Moses and is pronounced Mo-eez. Members of the family assume that they originated in Spain and migrated to France in the sixteenth century during the Spanish Inquisition.

At a time when the small-town Mississippi newspaper was weekly, when the telephone was not yet a common household item, and before the advent of radio and television, the only means for spreading the news of a funeral was through a printed funeral notice delivered by hand.

Two years before there was a public school system in Mississippi, Summit established the Peabody Public School in 1868. Among the directors of the school for nine years were two Jewish merchants, Isadore Moyse and Ben Hilborn.

Courtesy Peabody School

FUNERAL NOTICE

DIED

MOYSE—In New York, N. Y., Tuesday afternoon, August 17, 1915,

MRS. ROSALIE MOYSE,

wife of the late I. Moyse—aged 76 years.

The friends and acquaintances of the Moyse and Aronson families are respectfully requested to attend the Funeral Services, which will take place from the residence of Louis Aronson, Friday morning at 10 o'clock.

Summit, Miss., Aug. 18, 1915.

Courtesy Rosalie (Moyse) Raphael, Greenville

Isadore Kirschner stands in the front row, third from left, in his school picture at Peabody. He married Gertrude Eisenberg of Greenville, where the Kirschner family eventually moved.

109

A prominent pioneer citizen who served as the mayor of his town and organized the Bank of Summit, Sol Hyman lived in Summit for fifty years. His family owns a document showing his appointment as commissioner to represent Pike County at the Vienna Universal Exposition in 1873.

Russian-born Solomon "Sol" Hyman (1827–1910) left his native village of Weilga in 1850 to come to Mississippi at age twenty-three.

A prominent pioneer citizen who served as the mayor of his town and organized the Bank of Summit, Sol Hyman lived in Summit for fifty years. His family owns a document showing his appointment as commissioner to represent Pike County at the Vienna Universal Exposition in 1873.

Sol Hyman married Pauline Lichtenstein (1832–1916) in Holmesville, Mississippi, in 1856. From her modest picket-fenced house shown here, she went to the house Sol Hyman built in Summit.

The house of Mr. and Mrs. Sol Hyman, built in 1856, also pictured here on this page, is thought to be the oldest house still standing in Summit.

Photographs of the Lichtenstein home and of Mr. and Mrs. Sol Hyman courtesy Alfred E. Hiller, Metairie, Louisiana

110

A Summitonian, Mrs. John C. Covington wrote, "The Hymans came here from a land of oppression and found freedom of opportunity. They gained and in gratitude they contributed. They were valued citizens and they left their mark for the good."

Pauline and Sol Hyman pose with their family in front of their home in Summit on the occasion of their fiftieth wedding anniversary in 1906.

Courtesy Alfred E. Hiller, Metairie, Louisiana

Four of the five children (photograph c. 1870) of Solomon and Pauline Hyman, all born in Summit. From left to right, are Harris Hyman (1860–1934); Rogenia, who married Jonas Hiller, the son of a local family, Hertz and Julia (Cerf) Hiller; Alexander (1860–1934), who married

Courtesy Alfred E. Hiller, Metairie, Louisiana

The Hyman Mercantile Company invested $25,000 to help the town erect, according to the Summit Sun, *"the largest cotton compress in the world."*

Rosa Hart (1869–1955), a local girl; and Flora Hyman, who married Alfred Hiller, the son of Hertz and Julia (Cerf) Hiller. Thus, two sisters in the Sol Hyman family married two brothers in the Hertz Hiller family. The fifth Hyman child, who is not in this picture, is Eugene Hyman (1858–1915), who married Clara Pfeiffer (1868–1951), also a hometown girl.

The first business venture of Sol and Sam Hyman became known as the Hyman Mercantile and was one of the first stores in Summit. As it grew, it developed separate hardware, dry goods, and furniture departments. The cotton department added later handled up to 8,000 bales of cotton per season.

When Solomon Hyman retired from active business in 1897, his son Alexander became the president of the large cotton-buying firm, which served five counties.

The Hyman Mercantile Company invested $25,000 to help the town erect, according to the *Summit Sun,* "the largest cotton compress in the world."

Three Hiller brothers—Hertz, Matthew, and Abraham—came to Summit in the days of its infancy to enter the general merchandise business. Abraham had originally settled in Liberty, but sold his mercantile business to settle in Summit.

Hertz Hiller applied for a license to marry Julia (Cerf) Hiller in Liberty in 1854. The Hillers came from Hageneau, Alsace-Lorraine, to the United States in the late 1840s or early 1850s. Hertz Hiller saw service in the war and came back to his store in Summit, which was across the street from his friend, Sol Hyman, who originally came to town about the same time in 1856.

Alfred Hiller, the son of Hertz and Julia Hiller, is seen the year that he married Flora Hyman, the daughter of Sol and Pauline

Alfred Hiller.

Hyman. Their wedding in 1888 took place at the small, frame Ohaveh Shalom synagogue. Rabbi Max Heller, of Temple Sinai, New Orleans, officiated.

In the Alfred Hiller family portrait taken c. 1911 are, front row, left to right, Julian Hiller (1900–1975), Flora (Hyman) Hiller (1865–1944), Alfred Hiller, Sr., (1862–1927), and

Photographs courtesy Alfred E. Hiller, Metairie, Louisiana

Pauline (Lichtenstein) Hyman (1832–1916). In the back row, left to right, are Ray Hertz Hiller (1892–1947), Alfred Hiller, Jr., (1894–1910), Herbert Solomon Hiller (1890–1951), Irma (Hiller) Amberg (1889–1979), and her husband, Max Amberg.

Joe and Kate (Moak) Kirschner lived in this house built originally by Ben Hilborn. The inter-

weaving of old Southern Jewish families was common, clearly demonstrated in the example of the three Moak sisters. Kate Kirschner had two sisters. One sister, Carolyn, married Emanuel Levy of Summit. The other sister, Rosalie, married Isadore Moyse. Area boys married local girls and their combined families remained the focus of their lives.

Emanuel Levy (1830–1899), born in Buchsweiler, Alsace-Lorraine, came to Summit in the 1850s. In 1858 he married Carolyn Moak of Summit; later Levy served as a Confederate soldier during the war. The spacious house built by Emanuel and Carolyn (Moak) Levy still stands in Summit.

Courtesy *The Summit Sun*

112

The residence of John D. Jacobowsky. Records show that he bought and sold land in Amite County in 1852 and 1853. He made his start in business in Holmesville. As with other businessmen, when the center of activity moved to Summit because of the establishment of the railroad there, he, too, began business anew there, traveling between Holmesville and this home during the transition period.

The Charles Levy residence is still to be seen in Summit. Levy (1832–1909) was a soldier in the Confederate Army. The house was later occupied by the Perlinsky family, also of the Jewish community.

BROOKHAVEN

Brookhaven was incorporated in 1858 at about the same time when Jews began to arrive as peddlers or as merchants. The arrival of land purchasing agents for a railroad right-of-way and railroad construction brought settlers into the county.

Names such as H. Alcus, Emanuel Pfiefer, and Simon Kohlman appear in records of the city board, library, schools, and volunteer firemen. Abraham Lewinthal in 1889 became the first of three Jewish mayors to be elected. During his term of office he initiated the drive for the first public school building, which became affectionately called "The Little Red Schoolhouse."

Congregation B'nai Shalom (Hebrew: Children of Peace) was organized in 1894 and the temple was erected in 1896 at Chickasaw and South Church streets. The congregation was not large enough to have a rabbi on a full-time basis. This early photograph shows a steeple or bell tower. The bell is not characteristic of Jewish life and worship; the designer was evidently influenced by his building of churches. The steeple, however, has no bell.

Courtesy *Brookhaven Centennial Historical Program, 1859–1959*

113

According to the *Brookhaven Centennial Historical Program, 1859–1959* Milton Jacob Whitworth, a non-Jew, "had a consuming desire to make this part of Mississippi attractive to worthwhile settlers," and donated the land for the Jewish cemetery in 1861.

This painting of Natalie Wilson Cohn hangs in a prominent place in the Brookhaven public library. An inscription nearby reads, "In loving tribute to her long, outstanding, efficient service to this library and community."

Mrs. Cohn was joined by other citizens, including Max Lewinthal, in raising funds for founding a public library association (dues, $2.00 a year). After the library association's dream came true in 1910, Mrs. Cohn, at various times, served as president and board member.

Louis Cohn & Brothers general merchandise store, ". . . located in the building at the left, was established first in Monticello [Miss.] when three brothers, Louis, Emil, and David Cohn formed a partnership and in 1883 embarked in the mercantile business, transferring the business to Brookhaven in 1893 on Whitworth Avenue."

When the Commercial Bank began business in Brookhaven in 1887, Louis Cohn was its vice president.

The barber shop of the Inez Hotel was operated by a member of the Zwirn family who married Lotta Scherck, the daughter of Abraham and Sara Scherck.

Abraham Scherck, who was born in Posen, Germany, in 1838, came to the United States in 1851 at the age of thirteen through the port of New Orleans. He married Sara Green, who was born in 1840 in Gnessen, Germany. Both of them are buried in the Brookhaven Jewish cemetery.

Abraham went into the mercantile business in Brookhaven. His son Richard later joined him in the firm known as A. Scherck & Son. After the elder Scherck died in 1898, Richard built and operated the Inez Hotel, which was named after his daughter Inez.

Shown in this photograph are, left to right, three places of business owned and conducted by Jewish citizens of Brookhaven: the Inez Hotel, Bowsky Clothier, and the Lewinthal Mercantile.

The Abrams Mercantile Company. The lettering on the building in the center of the photograph just over the hood of the wagon spells ABRAMS. Cohn Abrams, born in Prussia in 1836, is among those listed who came to Brookhaven during the period of Reconstruction after the Civil War and who contributed toward the rebuilding of the life of the city. He and his wife Rusha had two sons, Isadore and Sam. The latter became the second Jewish mayor of Brookhaven. Two grandchildren of Cohn and Rusha still live in Brookhaven and conduct the original Abrams Mercantile Company. A great-grandson, Harold Samuels, became mayor of the City of Brookhaven in later years. Both Cohn and Rusha are buried in the Jewish cemetery of the city.

Scene, Cherokee Street in 1898. Background buildings are, at extreme left, a portion of the Lewinthal Drug Store and, at right, the Max Priebatsch store. Three of the people have been identified as Sam Zwirn, Ben Wilson, and Zollie Daniel, members of the Jewish community.

This two-story house on South Railroad Avenue was built for Mr. and Mrs. Richard T. Scherck and their family in 1896. Mr. Scherck later built the Inez Hotel and moved his family there. The house was purchased in 1906 by Judge P. Z. Jones.

CANTON

Because Canton was the terminal of several railroad companies, the town attracted Jewish merchants and became a focus for commercial activity. In the town square built around the courthouse there still stand buildings, constructed by pioneer merchants such as Loeb, Gross, Hesdorffer, Levy, Stein, Perlinsky, and Kaplan.

A small historical museum in the center of town includes the recorded history and some pictures of members of the Jewish community and of their place of worship.

Temple B'nai Israel was built on Academy and Liberty streets in 1874 and was paid for by monies raised at two benefit affairs at the Odd Fellows Hall. The first event netted $1,200. Rabbi Hecht was the first settled teacher and rabbi. The yellow fever epidemic caused a lapse in the course of services held at Temple B'nai Israel. During the last few years of the congregation, L. Lehmann served as the lay rabbi. It is

The yellow fever epidemic caused a lapse in the course of services held at Temple B'nai Israel. During the last few years of the congregation, L. Lehmann served as the lay rabbi. It is said, "He played the stock market by day and read services on Friday night."

said, "He played the stock market by day and read services on Friday night."

One of the first Jewish businessmen in Canton was Joseph Perlinsky. At the age of seventeen, in 1867, he opened his store during Reconstruction days. From an apprenticeship to a tailor in Poland he had come to an unknown cousin in Jackson, Julius Beck, and then to Canton, where there was no tailor and his services were needed.

Courtesy Lolita (Stein) Cohen, Jackson

Samson Wiener, who was born in 1834 in Heinsheim, Dukedom of Baden, Germany, married Caroline Forscheimer, whom he had met on the boat coming to the United States in 1852.

Prosperous, he brought his brother Henry from Poland to join him. The Perlinsky store stands in the town square as a memorial to the tailor who loved his community and his temple, where he was a charter member.

Leopold Stein was born in Ingenheim, Germany, in 1847. He married Frieda Lehmann, who had come to the United States at the age of fourteen to be with family in Canton. That city remained their home until he died in 1906. The hard-working couple operated a general store in downtown Canton.

Stein was especially friendly with Bishop Brunini of the Catholic Vicksburg diocese. The Bishop's mother Blanche was a Stein. He never forgot his cousins of another faith. When the Jewish congregation of Jackson, where a member of the Stein family lives, built a new temple, Bishop Brunini, in fine ecumenical gesture, made a gift of a *mezuzah** for the front door to the congregation.

*In response to two verses in Scripture (Deuteronomy 6:9 and 11:20), the observant Jew affixes a ceremonial item called *mezuzah* (from the Hebrew word for doorpost) to a doorpost of his home and of his synagogue.

After his marriage to Caroline in 1860, he worked in her Uncle Hirsch's general store in Sallis.

Weiner enlisted in 1861 and served in the Confederate Army, in the Mississippi Cavalry, for four years. He had several horses shot out from under him, but was never injured in any battle.

The Wiener family moved to Vaiden, Mississippi, and then to Winona in 1868. Canton's Jewish community and its temple turned out to be the inducement for moving to Canton.

In addition to his business, Samson took an after-hours job with the telegraph company. All his sons became expert telegraphers, so that they could relieve "Papa" and occasionally be his replacement at night. His full-time job eventually was as station master for the railroad.

Samson Wiener spoke five languages and so he also went to the various plantations around Madison County to teach French and German in the plantation schools. Further efforts to support his family involved work in a woodyard where he sold wood to householders and to the railroad. Samson Wiener died in Canton, Mississippi, in 1899.

Courtesy Dr. Julian Wiener, Jackson

Sam, William B., Ike, and Eli Wiener. The oldest of the boys, Ike (born in 1861 in Vaiden), became an expert telegrapher. In 1938, at the Chicago World's Fair, Ike took part in the dem-

onstrations sending and receiving telegraphic messages. William, born in 1863 in Vaiden, was the president of the Madison County Bank. He married Carrie Loeb, the daughter of Jacob and Mary (Gross) Loeb in Canton.

This house on Peace Street, formerly known as "the Loeb House," was torn down to make way for the building of the Canton City Hall. The snow scene was most unusual for the area.

Photographs courtesy Isabel Wile Goldman, Shreveport, Louisiana

The second view shows the Loeb family gathered at the wedding of Emily Loeb (the bride, seated at the far left) and Louis Wilde (standing at the far left) in 1891, at the home of her parents, Jacob and Mary Gross Loeb.

Jacob Loeb was born in Reichstoffer, France, in 1834. Two sources report different stories of his life.

According to the first source, Jacob Loeb left Europe for America to go to his sister, Sophie, who had married a prosperous gentleman by the name of Charles L. Gross who lived in Canton, Mississippi. Because the New Orleans port of entry was blockaded by the Union fleet during the

Civil War, his boat tried to land at Mobile, Alabama, but, again, was not able to approach the shore. The sailing vessel then let the passengers off in Mexico, where Jacob Loeb lived until after the Civil War. He then managed to peddle his way to Canton and his family.

The second account says that Jacob Loeb was en route to Mexico on a secret mission during the Civil War to arrange some financing for the Confederacy. When peace was declared and with no Confederacy government backing, he had to find his own way of returning to his family in Canton.

Jacob Loeb married Mary Gross, a half-sister of Charles L. Gross. The Loebs took an active part in Jewish community life in Canton.

Mary Gross Loeb was born in Strasbourg, Alsace Lorraine, in 1845. When her grandmother was ready to leave for America, she went to Mary's mother saying she "could bring one grandchild to this land of opportunity." She selected Mary, age three. Thus, Mary Gross came to the United States in 1848 and never saw her mother again. The grandmother and her charge lived in New York City near the Williamsburg bridge.

Mary Gross came as a young lady to Mississippi to visit her half-brother, C. L. Gross of Canton. She met and married Jacob Loeb, a merchant in that city. They had nine children; some of their descendants still live in that part of the state.

Mary Gross Loeb died in 1900. She and her husband Jacob are buried in the Canton Jewish cemetery.

The Loeb sisters. Standing, left to right, are Bertha, Florence, Emily, and Stella. Seated in the center is Carrie, who married William B. Wiener, Canton.

Charles L. Gross, born in Alsace-Lorraine in 1839, served in the Confederate Army with the 18th Mississippi Infantry, Barksdale Brigade. He married Sophie Loeb, a distant cousin who was also born in Alsace-Lorraine in 1839. He had a general store and was a highly respected businessman. Self-taught, he found time to read the best of literature and even read law books.

The home of Sophie and Charles Gross was filled with music, because all the girls were encouraged to take music lessons. Because of his high regard for education, he sent all four of their six surviving children to institutes of higher learning.

Those of his daughters who had special gifts were encouraged to develop them. Cylla and Sara played the piano. Mamie, the youngest, studied at the Peabody Conservatory in Baltimore. Flora, it is reported, was blessed with a fine voice.

Charles L. Gross was a charter member of Canton's Temple B'nai Israel. He died in 1898 and Sophie died in 1907. Both are buried in the Jewish cemetery in Canton.

Courtesy Elaine Ullman Lehmann, Natchez

The Charles L. Gross family. From left to right, first row: Dena, Albert, and Sara; second row: Sophie (mother), Mamie, and Charles (father); third row: Cylla, Samuel, and Flora.

Two sons of the Hesdorffers left Carthage to move to Jackson, but because there was a malaria epidemic in that city, they went instead to Canton.

Eugene (1865–1925) and Albert (1867–1935) opened a grocery store near the railroad on what local people called "the hollow." In 1905 they built the handsome E. & A. Hesdorffer building in the town square.

Eugene's wife Henrietta Goodman (1890–1971) had been placed as a child in the New Orleans Children's Orphanage when her mother died, because her father could not take care of the child. At age sixteen she went to be with a sister in Durant. Eugene Hesdorffer heard about the young visitor and made it his business to go to Durant to meet her.

It was only when Eugene Hesdorffer died that his widow learned his well-kept secret, as Canton people came to express their gratitude to their silent benefactor. Hesdorffer had, for many years, given groceries and help to needy families, and had wanted no recognition.

120

Albert, brother and business partner of Eugene, never married.

Mose Benjamin Hesdorffer (1825–1896) was born in Berlin and his wife Harriet (1840–1903)

Courtesy Dr. Eugene Hesdorffer, Jackson

came from Alsace-Lorraine. The couple came together to the United States where Hesdorffer started as a peddler. The Hesdorffers and their eight children lived in Carthage.

JACKSON

The city of Jackson, formerly LeFleur's Bluff, a trading post, was named in honor of Andrew Jackson in 1822. Because it was the state capital as well as a railroad center, Jackson played an important role during the Civil War. The city was the capital of the Confederacy until it was besieged in 1863 and the seat of government had to be moved. By 1865, Jackson had been rebuilt sufficiently to become the capital again.

Early Jewish settlers were John Hart, Lazarus Kahn, Isadore Strauss, Henry Strauss, Aaron Lehman, and H. Goodman. H. Goodman was the first president of Temple Beth Israel; some of the others conducted services. All were in the mercantile business.

Charles Ehrman was a member of the state

legislature, and Leopold Marks was sent to Jackson by Quitman County to serve as its first member of that body.

Congregation Beth Israel's first house of worship was built in 1861 on South State and South streets. The frame structure was burned by Federal troops when most of the city was sacked and burned.

Courtesy Harold Gotthelf, Jr., Jackson

A second synagogue was built on the same site in 1867, and it was destroyed by fire in 1874. By the following year, a new sanctuary was built and dedicated. When this structure was sold and dismantled in 1940, it was the oldest religious edifice in the capital city.

John Hart, whose family name was changed from Hertz, was born in Kuppenheim, Germany, in 1832. He was the son of Joseph and Bertha Hertz and came to the United States in 1846 with his boyhood friend Benjamin Kuppenheimer. The friend went to Chicago and became the well-known clothing manufacturer. John Hart went to Jackson and was employed at first by a local butcher, George Muh, for $10 a month.

When war broke out, he joined Company A, Sixth Mississippi Brigade of the Confederate Army in 1861. After the war, Hart was convinced that Jackson had a great future and began to buy property in the area. He eventually became the largest taxpayer of city property in Jackson.

In 1866 he formed J. & B. Hart and Company. That same year he married Julia Lehman of Brownsville, Mississippi. John Hart served as

Courtesy *History of Mississippi*, Dunbar Rowland

Photographs courtesy Joan (Ascher) Cahn, Meridian

John Hart

Mr. and Mrs. Joseph Ascher

president of Beth Israel Congregation for twenty years.

Benjamin and Phillip Hart left the home of their father, Joseph Hertz, in Kuppenheim, Germany, to follow their brother John, who had preceded them to the United States. (Hertz is German for "heart," changed later to Hart.)

Joseph Ascher, son of Melanie and Gershon Ascher, was born in Alsace in 1855. When he was twenty-one years old, his parents sent him to Melanie's brothers, John, Phillip, and Benjamin Hart of Jackson.

Joseph started out as a drummer and began to buy real estate. His philosophy was to buy but never sell land or property. In 1885, he married Blanche Simon, who was born in Louisiana in 1866. She and her family lived in Kosciusko, Mississippi.

The Joseph Ascher family is pictured with grandmother, Marie (Feibelman) Simon in their home, c. 1900, on Amite Street. The youngest child, sitting on the floor, is Isaac Simon Ascher.

122

Aaron Lehman, a pioneer merchant in Jackson, was one of the founders of Temple Beth Israel.

Isadore Lehman, born in Jackson in 1879, was the son of Aaron Lehman and is seen seated, lower left, on the floor for a first grade class picture.

In 1891, when Isadore Lehman was twelve years old, he began his business career by representing a Memphis laundry in Jackson. He established the Jackson Steam Laundry in 1904 and remained its president until his death.

Born in 1879 and a native Jacksonian who loved his city, Isadore Lehman was involved in every facet of community life. The following is an

Born in 1879 and a native Jacksonian who loved his city, Isadore Lehman was involved in every facet of community life. The following is an incomplete list: president of the Jackson Chamber of Commerce, president of Beth Israel congregation, president of the Mississippi Chamber of Commerce, president of Hinds County Red Cross, president of the Jackson school board.

incomplete list: president of the Jackson Chamber of Commerce, president of Beth Israel congregation, president of the Mississippi Chamber of Commerce, president of Hinds County Red Cross, president of the Jackson school board.

123

Although he lived most of his years in Vicksburg and worked with his brothers Henry and Albert in the large family business of meat markets throughout the city, "Jake" Ehrman, in his later years, was the owner of this Jackson meat market on the southeast corner of Pearl and President streets from 1890 to 1920.

Courtesy *A Special Kind of Place*, Carroll Brinson (W. M. Dalehite, photograph editor)

The Emporium, billed as Jackson's leading department store, had as its executive officer Simon Seelig Marks.

The father of the three Ehrman men was Charles Ehrman, who served in the state legislature.

Jake Ehrman was, like his father, interested in politics and was a good friend of United States Senator James K. Vardaman.

Jake is buried alongside his parents, Charles and Clara (Ehlbert) Ehrman, in the Jackson Jewish cemetery.

The Emporium, billed as Jackson's leading department store, had as its executive officer Simon Seelig Marks. He was born in Meridian in 1888 the son of Israel and Hettie (Ritterman) Marks. After attending Phillips Academy at Andover and

graduating from Yale, he worked with Marks, Rothenberg & Company in Meridian. In 1917, Marks married Josephine Hyams, a daughter of Henry and Violet (Strauss) Hyams of Jackson.

An active man, he was a director of the Mississippi Merchants Association, vice president of the Jackson Chamber of Commerce, and a Kiwanian. He was appointed to the post of state director for the National Emergency Council for Mississippi during the days of the Franklin Delano Roosevelt administration.

This Jackson-born "sailor boy," Julian B. Feibelman, was destined to become a nationally acclaimed rabbi known for his ecumenical work in New Orleans. He was a graduate of Millsaps College in Jackson and was ordained by the Hebrew Union College in Cincinnati.

The leadership of this rabbi was put to an unusual test when Dr. Ralph Bunche, a recipient of the Nobel Peace Prize for his role as mediator in the dispute between mid-eastern Jews and Arabs, agreed to speak in pre-integration times in New Orleans. Dr. Bunche, a black gentleman who served as a United States diplomat to the United Nations, stipulated that there must be no segregation of races at this lecture. Despite the committee's frantic search, no auditorium in compliance with the conditions set was available.

Rabbi Feibelman went to the board of trustees of his Sinai Congregation for permission to use its large temple for that meeting.

A large crowd filled the temple. Jews and Christians, blacks and whites sat together and listened to a superb address by Dr. Bunche. There was no trouble; there were no incidents. After the meeting, the people of New Orleans, the press, and civic leaders praised Rabbi Feibelman and the congregation of Temple Sinai for having the courage to live up to their principles.

The Feibelman family of Jackson included Abraham and Eva (Beck) Feibelman and their two children, Sayde Feibelman (later Hart) and young Julian, (1897–1980), whose book, *The Making of a Rabbi*, appeared posthumously.

When Moise Cohen came from Vaslui, Romania, in 1889 at age fifteen, to Jackson, he worked as a drummer or peddler. In 1898, his brother Sam arrived at age twenty to join his brother in the newly opened men's and ladies' apparel store to be known as Cohen Brothers.

A traveling salesman from Memphis introduced Moise to his sister-in-law, Etta Cohen. Shortly afterwards the salesman introduced Etta's sister, Nell, to Sam Cohen. The Cohen girls did not even have to change their names when they married the Cohen boys.

An unusual relationship developed since the two couples lived in the same house—peacefully—on East Fortification Street. Their children were double cousins and they speak of a jolly home full of fun.

Moise and Etta Cohen and Sam and Nell Cohen together celebrated fifty years of marriage in 1959.

Epilogue

When Mrs. Turitz and I came to Meridian, Mississippi, in 1971, for me to serve the Jewish congregation in a somewhat retirement capacity, the dread circumstances of the mid-1960s were a thing of the past and our six years there were happy ones.

The masthead beneath the name of the local newspaper read: "The New South," and that it was insofar as we knew.

We experienced no vestiges of "The Klan's Campaign Against the Jews" nor did we witness any obvious hatred of the Afro-American people such as were reported to have taken place during the 1960s and related so skillfully by Jack Nelson in his recent book, *Terror in the Night*. Neither did zealous, Christian evangelicals make our people uncomfortable.

During our time in Meridian, I. A. Appelbaum, a former president of our congregation, served as mayor of the city of Meridian for two terms.

Dr. Hobert Kornegay, Jr., a Black dentist, served as an alderman.

Schools and buses were integrated.

The membership of the ministerial association consisted of whites and blacks, Protestants and Catholics and me, the Jew. I served as program chairman for two years and was to serve as president my last year there. (Actually, I was not able to follow through because of an illness.)

The ladies of the churches and of our synagogue formed a citywide interfaith organization that met several times during the year. At one of their functions, I, the rabbi, was privileged to be the main speaker, and the affair took place, yes, at the large First Baptist Church. Twice during our years there, the organization met at our Temple.

The local television station allotted a fifteen-minute space each weekday morning for a religious program, and the clergymen of all denominations were invited to participate. Thus, a minister, priest, or rabbi had the opportunity to present five programs every eleventh week. Again, this included black and white, Protestant and Catholic and Jew.

One year, prior to the Passover season, the ladies of the Temple Sisterhood invited the clergymen of all denominations to attend a model Seder service and meal. There was a large attendance, and response was receptive and enthusiastic. Present also was the editor of the newspaper, and he followed up with an editorial appraising the event in a positive manner and inspiring the spirit of brotherhood.

We pay tribute to the Mississippi rabbis who preceded our coming into the state and who fought bravely for human rights.

Without denying or overlooking the turbulence of the previous periods of discontent of Mississippi history, we consider ourselves fortunate to have been there in a time described by the newspaper as "The New South" and during which time and after we were impelled to research and produce this book.

Leo E. Turitz, Rabbi

Bibliography

The South

Dinnerstein, Leonard and Mary Dale Palsson, eds. *Jews in the South*. Baton Rouge: Louisiana State University Press, 1973.

Evans, Eli N. *The Provincials*. New York: Atheneum, 1973.

Golden, Harry. *Our Southern Landsman*. New York: G. P. Putnam's Sons, 1974.

Kaganoff, Nathan N. and Melvin I. Uropfsky, eds. *Turn to the South, Essays on Southern Jewry*. Charlottesville: Southern Jewish Historical Society and University Press of Virginia, 1976.

Korn, Bertram Wallace. *The Early Jews of New Orleans*. Waltam, Massachusetts: American Jewish Historical Society, 1969.

Korn, Bertram Wallace. *American Jewry and the Civil War*. Philadelphia: Jewish Publication Society, 1951.

Marcus, Jacob R., ed. *Memoirs of American Jews, 1775–1865*. 3 vols. Philadelphia: Jewish Publication Society, 1955.

Schmier, Louis, ed. *Reflections of Southern Jewry: The Letters of Charles Wessolowsky, 1878–1879*. Macon, Georgia: Mercer University Press, 1982.

Mississippi

Brieger, James F. *Hometown, Mississippi*. Jackson: Mississippi Department of Archives and History, 1980.

Dollard, John. *Caste and Class in a Southern Town*. New Haven: Yale University Pres, 1937.

Garner, James Wilford. *Reconstruction in Mississippi*. New York: Macmillan Co., 1901.

Map Collection. Mississippi Department of Archives and History, Jackson.

Postal, Bernard and Lionel Koppman. *American Jewish Landmarks*, Vol. 2. New York: Fleet Press, n.d.

Rowland, Dunbar. *History of Mississippi*, Vol. 3. Jackson: S. J. Clarke Publishing Company, 1925.

Sheppard, J. S. *Mississippi State Gazetteer and Shippers' Guide, 1866*. Memphis: J. S. Sheppard, 1866.

Wall, E. G. *Hand-Book of the State of Mississippi*. Board of Immigration and Agriculture. Jackson: Clarion Steam Printing Establishment, 1885.

Wilner, W. "Mississippi" in *The Jewish Encyclopedia*, Vol. 12. New York: Funk and Wagnalls Co., 1916.

Wolf, Simon. *The American Jew as Patriot, Soldier, and Citizen*, N.p.: Levytype Co., 1895.

Work Projects Administration (WPA). *Inventory of the Church and Synagogue Archives of Mississippi, Jewish Congregations and Organizations*. Jackson: Mississippi Department of Archives and History, 1940.

Individual Cities and Towns of Mississippi

Brookhaven

Brookhaven Centennial Incorporated. *Brookhaven Centennial Historical Program, 1859–1959*.

The Daily Leader.

Clarksdale

Tolochko, J. Gerson. *Beth Israel Anniversary Issue*. Clarksdale, 1939.

Tolochko, J. Gerson. *Judaism*. Clarksdale, 1939. Mimeo.

Columbus

Lipscomb, William L. *History of Columbus [Mississippi]*. Birmingham, 1909.

Mitlin, Luceille L. *Migration of the Families of Jews Presently Living in Columbus, Starkville and Aberdeen, Missis-

sippi*. Mitchell Memorial Library, Mississippi State College, 1972. Mimeo.

Greenville

Goldstein, Nathan. "Golden Jubilee of the Hebrew Union Temple." Greenville *Daily Democrat*, January 12, 1871.

Solomon, Herman W. *The Jews of Greenville, Mississippi*. N.p., 1950s [?]. Mimeo.

Hattiesburg

Brodey, Arthur. "B'nai Israel Congregation." The Hattiesburg *American*, September 19, 1936.

Jackson

Davis, Frances. "Historic Temple Here Yields to Growth." Jackson *Daily News*, May 12, 1940.

Power, Kate M. "A History of the Jewish Congregation in Jackson." Jackson *Daily News*, June 7, 1936.

Meridian

Barksdale, John. *Citizens of Color in Meridian, Mississippi, Progress Report, 1831–1962*. Meridian, 1962. Privately printed.

Croom, W. G. *Complete History and Business Directory of the City of Meridian, Miss., 1882–83*. Chas. P. Dement, 1882.

Desha, Robert, compiler. *A Business and Complete Directory of the City of Meridian*. Meridian: Camel and Powell, Star Printing House, 1873.

Dokey Drum and Bugle Corps, compiler. *The Original Meridian Quiz Program*. Meridian: Interstate Printers, Inc., 1941.

Edmiston, Fred W., compiler. *Directory of the City of Meridian, Miss., 1866–1872*. Typescript, 1967.

Edmiston, Fred W. A study of Marion, Mississippi, for *The Lauderdale Repub-

lican. Typescript, 1854–1856.

Grauel, W. B. *History of Meridian and Lauderdale County. The Meridian Star*, 1947. Booklet.

Gray, William. F. *Meridian Illustrated: 1904, A Comprehensive Picture of the Metropolis of Mississippi in its Historial, Civic, Social, Industrial and Commercial Aspects*. N.p.: Tell Farmer, 1904.

Maloney, T. V., ed. *Meridian, Mississippi City Directory, Metropolis of the Southwest: A Descriptive, Historical, and Statistical Review: Industry, Development, and Enterprise, 1888*. Privately printed.

Richardson, L. W., ed. *Meridian, Miss., Southern Cities Illustrated*. New Orleans: C. W. Forbes, 1894.

Runnels, F. M., compiler. *Illustrated Handbook of Meridian, Mississippi*. Meridian Board of Trade and Cotton Exchange, 1907.

Shank, George Kline, Jr. "Meridian: A City at Birth, During the Civil War, and in Reconstruction." Master's thesis, Mississippi State University, 1961.

Shannon and Andrews. *Business Directory of the City of Meridian*, 1884.

Snowden, E. G. "The Meridian Campaign, Sherman in Mississippi, Feb. 1864. Master's thesis, University of Alabama, 1976.

Stevenson and Company Machinery Agency. *Meridian, Mississippi, The Most Important Town in the State*. Meridian: Chas. P. Dement, 1885.

Natchez

"bw." "Temple B'nai Israel." Natchez, n.d. Carbon copy of typescript.

"Translations of the Spanish Records," Book C, Chancery Clerk, Adams County.

Forman, Samuel S. *Narrative of a Journey Down the Ohio and Mississippi in 1789– 90*. N.p., Robert Clarke and Co., 1888.

James, Clayton. *Antebellum Natchez*. Baton Rouge: Louisiana State University Press, 1968.

McCormick, C. N., ed. *Natchez, Mississippi, On Top, Not Under the Hill. The Natchez Daily Democrat*, 1887.

Moore, Edith Wyatt. "Temple B'nai Israel." Natchez, 1940. Typescript.

Mygatt, A. & Co. *Business Directory*. Natchez, 1858.

The City of Natchez. Natchez, 1881.

Natchez *Courier*.

Natchez *Democrat*.

Natchez *Evening Gazette*.

Natchez *Mississippi Free Trader*.

Power, Major Steve, ed. *The Memento: Old and New Natchez, 1700 to 1897*. Natchez: Major Steve Power, 1897.

Rattray, Dave. *The City of Natchez, Mississippi, 1881*. Natchez: Rattray Publishing Company, 1881.

Reber, Thomas. *Proud Old Natchez*. Natchez, 1909.

Shields, Joseph Dunbar. *Natchez, Its Early History*. N.p.: John P. Morton and Company, 1930.

Tuttle, A. C. *Natchez Directory, for 1877– 78*. Natchez: Tuttle Publishing, 1877.

Port Gibson

Douglas, Ed Polk. *Architecture in Claiborne County, Mississippi*. James H. Stone, editor. Jackson: Mississippi Department of Archives and History, 1974.

Headly, Katy McCaleb, ed. *Claiborne County, Mississippi: The Promised Land*. Port Gibson—Claiborne County Historical Society. Baton Rouge: Moran Industries, Inc., 1976.

Summit

Conerly, Luke Ward. *History of Pile County. The Summit Sun*, anniversary editions. April 4, 1940; November 29, 1945; April 10, 1958.

Vicksburg

Battaile, J. F., and H. P. Chapman. *Picturesque Vicksburg*. Vicksburg Printing and Publishing Co., 1895.

Philipsborn, Gertrude. *The History of the Jewish Community of Vicksburg*. Vicksburg, 1969. Mimeo.

Tuttle, A. C., ed. *Complete Directory of the City of Vicksburg*. Vicksburg: Rogers and Groom, 1879.

In and About Vicksburg, 1890. N.P.: United Service Publishing Co., n.d.

Woodville

Dreyfus, A. Stanley, ed. *Henry Cohen, Messenger of the Lord*. New York: Bloch Publishing Co., 1963.

"The Jewish Synagogue." *The Woodville Republican*, July 19, 1924.

Marcus, Jacob R., ed. *Memoirs of American Jews, 1775–1865*. Philadelphia: Jewish Publication Society, 1955.

Schappes, Morris U., ed. *A Documentary History of the Jews in the United States, 1654–1875*. Charleston: The Citadel Press, 1950; revised, 1952.

Schwartzman, Sylvan D. *Reform Judaism— Then and Now*. New York: Union of American Hebrew Congregations, 1971.

Sklare, Marshall. *America's Jews*. New York: Random House, 1971.

Wischnitzer, Mark. *Visas to Freedom: The History of HIAS* (Hebrew Immigrant Aid Society). New York: World, 1956.

General References

Birmingham, Stephen. *Our Crowd: The Great Jewish Families of New York*. New York: Harper and Row, 1967.

Blau, Joseph L. and Salo W. Baron, eds. *The Jews of the United States, 1790– 1840: A Documentary History*. 3 vols. New York: Columbia University Press and the Jewish Publication Society, 1963.

Blau, Joseph L., ed. *Reform Judaism: A Historical Perspective*. New York: KTAV Publishing Co., 1973.

Durant, Will and Ariel. *The Lessons of History*. New York: Simon and Schuster, 1968.

Engelman, Uriah Sevi. *Jewish Statistics in the U. S. Census of Religious Bodies, 1850–1936*. N.p., Jewish Social Studies, 9, 1947.

Feingold, Henry L. "The Land of Promise." *Keeping Posted*, 23, October, 1977.

Glanz, Rudolf. *Jews in Relation to the Cultural Milieu of the Germans in America up to the Eighteen Eighties*. Booklet, 1947.

Gumbiner, Joseph. *Isaac Mayer Wise: Pioneer of American Judaism*. New York: Union of American Hebrew Congregations, 1959.

Handlin, Oscar. *Adventure in Freedom*. New York: McGraw-Hill, 1954.

Heller, James G. *Isaac Mayer Wise: His Life, Work, and Thought*. New York: Union of American Hebrew Congregations, 1965.

Hertzberg, Arthur. *The French Enlightenment and the Jews*. New York: Columbia University, 1968.

Hirt-Manheimer, Aron, ed. *A Century of German Jewish Immigration*. N.p., n.d.

Janowsky, Oscar I., ed. *The American Jew*. Philadelphia: Jewish Publication Society, 1964.

Karp, Abraham J. "The Flow of German Jews: 1830–1880." *Golden Door to America: The Jewish Immigrant Experience*. New York: Viking, 1976.

Lowenthal, Marvin. *The Jews of Germany: A Story of Sixteen Centuries*. Philadelphia: Jewish Publications Society, 1936.

Manners, Ande, *Poor Cousins*. New York: Coward, McCann & Geoghegan, 1972.

Marcus, Jacob R., ed. *American Jewry*. New York: Union College Press, 1959.

Marcus, Jacob R. *The American Jewish Woman, 1654–1980*. New York: American Jewish Archives and KTAV Publishing Co., 1981.

Marcus, Jacob R. *The American Jewish Woman: A Documentary History*. New York: American Jewish Archives and KTAV Publishing Co., 1981.

Index